THE CARNAL MYTH

By the same author

Because I Was Flesh
Bottom Dogs
Can These Bones Live
The Sorrows of Priapus

THE CARNAL MYTH

A Search into Classical Sensuality

EDWARD DAHLBERG

SIGNATURE SERIES

CALDER AND BOYARS · LONDON

First published in Great Britain in 1970
by Calder and Boyars Ltd
18 Brewer Street London W1

© *Edward Dahlberg, 1968*

SBN 7145 0694 X cloth edition
SBN 7145 0695 8 paper edition

Printed in Great Britain by
Thomas Nelson (Printers) Ltd
London and Edinburgh

To Harold Billings
and
William R. Holman

INTRODUCTION

I HAVE PUT OFF composing this pelting introduction because my heart is lazy, and besides, I never suppose I have a single thought in my head. As a result, there have been weeks of waste, shame, and dross. One of the greatest fears I have had is that I shall be no more than a miserable proser. Then, I have not had the courage to look at this parcel of the book *The Carnal Myth* in a decade. (A moiety was published by New Directions in 1957, and bore the title *The Sorrows of Priapus*.)

My inclination has been to comb numerous leaves of erudite volumes or to do anything except even slubber over what I had written. So I softly ambled from one sage of literature to another. Nothing helped. To write is a humiliation. You are spiritless because you believe what you have put on paper is a scrawl. But to do nothing is a fell yoke. What other causes are there to make a book? Will it not, in a short space of God's hours, be as neglected as the sheep pasture of Anaxagoras?

My entire life always has hung by the thread of Ariadne. Each day I am apparelled in dust and stupidity. A demon forces me to step out of the mean shoals of satiety and refuse that which comes of velleity. The average accept their limits. I take up my pen, a trident, to rake away all the marine shrubs and bracken in man's obscure and watery depths. I could say I write because I will die. Or, I do this to understand myself. But I suspect I cannot abide the nihilistic idol *no-thing* any more than the Lord could abide the *void*. Have I the smallest hope of moulding the words as an acolyte of the seminal *logoi*? I know nothing, that is sure, but I do my best to record it with equatorial feeling.

One day, walking through the stricken valley of Hinnom called New York, I met a dullard of our humbug Arcady who felt he must burst should he not disclose this secret to me: "I find your work diverting." (Stendhal tells us that after the *Cid* appeared, Corneille was nothing for M. le Marquis de Danjeau but a "good fellow."

Admit it, demands my abyss, the writer's occupation, according to Ben Jonson, is a "sacrament of misery." To be truthful is to dwell in a tomb described as society.

Though I peddle words, groans, or my clouts—or what Blake named imagination, the "rotten rags of memory"— who will buy or store them? "Mantua delights in Vergil, Verona in Catullus," is a sentence out of Ovid. But what hamlet or city commemorates the American poet? The Philister will never realize that a land without bards is Job's Sherd.

No matter, I decline to lie down with the logicians of Mammon or the harebrains of belles lettres and nuzzle fame as the sows do acorns. Speak not to me of reputation or money, for what cruel nights lie on my head. Furthermore, all can be purchased in the literary public stews, or as Wyatt put it: "In wrong preisying is all his craft and arte." There are many quandaries: We are not producing gallants, amorists, picaros, or even passionate simpletons.

Perversity is the simpering seraph of the age. "For hateful to me even as the gates of Hell is he that hideth one thing in his heart and uttereth another" (Homer). The aim of the poetaster is to be new, symptom of his dotage. As Giordano Bruno says: "Call bread, bread, wine, wine, the head, the head, the foot, the foot." The froward hackney canonizes jargon and the up-to-date neologies of the squalid tradesmen and gombeen man. The Parnassian trimmers have broken the vertebrae of the language, and that is a sin against holy English.

What is the difference between the churlish colloquialisms of the guttersnipe and the solecisms of the pedagogue who is an ambulatory textbook? Literature is under the tyranny of the sharpers and the Grub Street dwarf. I detest the rabble in all places, and cannot tolerate the literary, the intellectual, and the academic sheep. "The crowd is untruth," declared Kierkegaard, and Baudelaire announced he was no member of the brotherhood of prostitutes.

Since my prentice to letters, I have belonged to the sodality of one. All my days I have searched for the lost Atlantis of an unattainable Golden Epoch; yet my lot has been the bleak shingle of Patagonia, and my diet often less than that of the natives who subsist on rotten blubber and shellfish, with the mizzling weather in my desponding knees.

Could I have lived otherwise? One's character is his meal and hard hap. Nobody has a choice, but if he does not take it, he is a poltroon.

I was born in the Barren Grounds, where love is stunted as a lichen. What passes for erudition, but is void of affection, is hemlock. Therefore, I live in exile among the frigid swarm. Long ago I would have perished had I not pined for absolutes, though they do not exist. (It is told by Eunapius, the ancient biographer, that Plotinus saw the Absolute four times.)

But utility is our national shibboleth: the savior of the American businessman is *fact* and his uterine half-brother, *statistics*. I defy both. What is practical impedes the glories of the pensive animal, man. Why should I care a whit about a gammon of crude particulars that are no more than a miasmal, crapulous room, an orgulous, shut door, or moldy, voiceless steps?

Is this a negative proem? Then I reply, those who cringe before an apocalyptic negation are dissemblers. I see what I must, and that is prophetic. Moreover, I am unable to suffer mean and shoaly limits, and know that the Ursa Major of my life is the imagination. "The mouths of the poets are refreshed by the waters of Pieria," declared Ovid. Would I could claim that the altars of Plotinus have not yet grown cold. Woe, it is a dead, garbaged day, but the labor for the mythic hour must be continued. What other work or refection is there for the scribe exiled in his own land? Whilst we live we must toil for the sublime or be the scullions of the vulgus.

The sun is gone, and there is dusk in my mad heart, but I shall sing a stave of denials far better than the pragmatic yeas of the Caliban of American literature. Chant I must, though there is a rand of ice in my spirit.

It is an age of separation, and men apart from others abhor those they cannot touch. Each one is graved, and this is the devil he calls *together*. Although he winces, he must take the hazard and shake the hand of another; a dirty sepulchre himself, he considers everyone else unclean. He babbles about sanitation, the toilet, the art of plumbing, the sewage, as if the cloaca were the Garden of Silenus, though the cities stink and there is ordure in the gutters and on the pavements. He takes unto his bosom the cat the abominable Egyptian worshipped, but declines to be close to a human being. But if we do not exchange one another's germs, we will rot of indifference, the worst plague since the time of Thucydides in Athens. Such a mortal infection is this that not a starved dog will approach it.

All these contradictions wound my whole blood. As a writer, I am benumbed by what the grammarians refer to as American literature, which is an exercise in elocution. Alone, and cold as Lake Titicaca, the flowers around its marge are my aspic doubts. Deprivation has become my seer. More than a sigh ago, I saw there were two alternatives: either bow down to Baal Peor, the idol of comfort or hew obsidian truths out of solitude and mountains. The guerdon has been penury, dismal fits of obscurity (and the sole consolation, "Oblivion cannot be hired" of Sir Thomas Browne), and now the distant applause of unfamiliar readers who seek the Colchian fleece guarded by a pair of dragons, the world and Mammon.

Let us examine the quiddity of the perplexity, *form*. A Chinese scholar of the philosophy of painting has stated it this way: "To learn to draw bamboo, take a branch and cast its shadow on a white wall on a moonlight night: then its true outline can be obtained." I say, imitate Longinus, a walking library, and cull your English from Wyatt, Surrey, Sir Walter Raleigh, Robert Burton, Izaak Walton, Ben Jonson, Jonathan Swift, Addison, and Steele. Go everywhere for the humblest honey for intelligence, never ceasing to champ the analects of Heraclitus, Xenophanes, Empedocles, Callimachus, Martial, and Horace.

Ultimately, it is only style that is important. Unless this is rightly understood, a book will be a blizzard of grammar. Spite of any didactic motive in the mind of the inventor of a poem or an essay, he is incapable of divulging the truth in a boorish iambic or prose. He may convey information, the cash logic of the professor in our colleges of astral nonsense.

Where can the naïve reader, misguided by critical loggerheads, look for the viaticum to nourish him? Often he sups on aesthetics, the apotheosis of the colon and the caesura, and is far from Rabelais's "the honest manna of literature."

As for me, I would rather walk among the Amorites, or idle in the olive yards of Sumer with the goddess of amours, Astarte; for I am an anachronism who must reflect willynilly this putrid century. O give me gutwort, for I am at odds with this pocky era, Let the dunderheads consider me among the dead, for up until 1964 I myself had exclaimed: "I have been writing posthumously for a generation."

But all is not snow, rain, and hail. How jubilant I am when a soft etesian gale blows against my sere branches. Then I am Hector, who is tender as the mulberry, and when I tremble, I can grasp daybreak flittering on the *Cordilleras* of the Andes. Famished, I ache for earth, a scrub oak, a blade of grass, a cockle, a sand dune, and mourn for the

American terrain devoured by the triple-throated Cerberus, the cartel. I dote on headlands and coves, Hakluyt's voyages, the Journals of Joutel, Pigafetta's Magellan. My hopes are trussed up as I peruse Xenophon's *Anabasis*, the march of Coronado through feral Kansas, Garcilaso de la Vega's *Royal Commentaries*. One other balm I need: myths which eased the aging Aristotle.

May I disclose how I commenced this *boke*? In 1951, I perceived that the rituals of the New World are not inferior to those of Hellas, Babylon, Egypt, or Rome. What is in the *Tibetan Book of the Dead* or in the *Rig-Veda* that cannot be found in the *Popol Vuh* of the Quiché Maya?

Looking for my identity in our indigenous ground, I rummaged through the *Orbe Novo* of the Franciscan monk Peter Martyr, the letters of Cortez to Charles the Fifth; ransacked the sundry chronicles about de Soto; studied millenniums of pages regarding the Indians. Nor did I eschew Pausanias, Athenaeus and Diogenes Laertius, the dialogues pertaining to the sainted ruffian of the Stoics, Diogenes, or the prodigies of Ptolemy's cartography.

I had not the effrontery of my contemporary pismires who call Herodotus and Strabo liars. No doubt Sir John Mandeville's *Travels*, an admixture of Pliny's *Natural History*, Marco Polo's peregrinations, and the annals of the Bible, are specious, but still of worth to those whose faculties are kindled by cabbalistical speculations. Nor could I spew forth the draff of the Seven Cities of Cibola, bequeathed to us by Fray Marcos. There is much superstition in knowledge, and the imaginative errors of Theophrastus and Dioscorides, the Greek herbalist, are precious food for the mind.

After poring over the *relaciós* of the Jesuits who came to

the American wilderness in the sixteenth and seventeenth centuries, I realized that ill fortune lards the destiny of men. Who can muse upon the disasters of Panphilo de Narváez or the pilgrimage of Cabeza de Vaca, who walked naked from the Atlantic to the Rio de Palmas (the Rio Grande), without understanding that suffering is the Buddha of all flesh?

Man's lodestone is disgrace, infamy, hunger, and ship-wreck. Thousands of Spanish soldiers and conquistadors drowned in the vast sea of darkness, and those who survived ate their companions who had died.

(There is another conflict within me I cannot resolve: I bless poverty, though I require lucre; but when I smell it, I behave as the horse whose nostrils are offended by the camel.)

Occupied with Suetonius's *Twelve Caesars* and the *Annals* of Tacitus, I saw I was drawn to the pravity of man, since I learned that the lubricous bill of fare of Messalina, the greed of Cleopatra, and the knack of dissembling of the Emperor Tiberius and his twelve houses of lust at Capri taught me more than the moral maxims of Seneca.

When I started *The Sorrows of Priapus*, I felt it was not possible to be a good scribe without knowing the rites of Isis and Osiris and the erotic Serapeum of Mnevis and Apis and pondering the significance of Thammuz, the phallic idol for whom the women of Israel wept by the walls of Jerusalem. Nor could I expunge the repulsive sacrifices of the Aztecs from the *Sorrows*.

A baleful thought oppressed me: Is the appetite for gore essential to the inquisitorial intellect? Heraclitus revealed that war is the father of progress, and I want no part of martial citizens, and loathe progress.

Such is skin that I acknowledge that evil is a savant superior to virtue. Of the latter, I possess only that which would fill the tiniest space of a pedant's footnote. Still, may no one surmise that I lack principles or hanker for debaucheries. Alas, good deeds do not replenish the eyes, the arms, or succor the feet. Much to my dismay, I have discovered that he who helps a person may often harm him.

Self-revelation is a heavy Petrine doubt hanging about my neck. That is what writing is. I fume away my gloom and imagine I am gaining a knowledge of my nature, and that is sufficient to make a Goya cower. Despite this, in every book, good or ill, I did my utmost never to be the cony-catcher of the reader, for as Euripides has it: "No lie ever grows old."

After I had finished *The Sorrows of Priapus*, I had no idea what I had done. An author has nothing except an animal conjecture about his toil. Without cant, I assert that I do not understand how I have put my books together nor comprehend anybody I have encountered.

Living in the age of separation, I have a clandestine wish I can not repress: not having written this work to instruct others, I hope it will be a remedy of sorts for those who are broken, my sole kin, wherever they are. The archives in ancient Alexandria, containing the poems and scholia of the Greeks, were alluded to as a healing library. I made apothegms, never failing to be concerned with form first and last, but prayed after they were framed they might be a scanty value to those remote hermits, dying in the Arctic Circle of the literati. Had I the dung of the musk ox as fuel in the frozen regions to warm them?

All this is a paradox. Absurd. How could I claim I could concoct a simple for others? Bled to the quick by the briars and thorns that punish us, I cite Pascal, who said that man is as automatic as he is intellectual. I go farther, saying he is wholly unconscious. Were this not so, who would do what he has done? We grieve all the days of our lives because of our mistakes. What, pray, do we gather from them? Do I go astray? Provided the poet has austerely disciplined himself, he may then work as if he were asleep. Ch'ing, an artisan, wrote: "After the fifth day of a devotion [to my work], I am oblivious of fame or blame. On the seventh day, I am unconscious even of my own limbs." Should he think he is awake, he is only distracted and not at all vigilant.

He who is of the faith that he has a thousand ideas to give to others is a noddy or, far worse, astute. Each morning I go to my desk as if I were making ready to walk to the gallows. This I must do or live dead, for when I am sterile as the marshes about Cadiz, I am utterly bored and beside myself. Would that I might grow my foliage twelve months a year and be verdurous as the district of Elephantine, where neither vines nor figs lost their leaves.

Have I spoken too much of the travails of a scribe? Yet silence shrouds my skin. But one more flinty truth I have to utter: A reluctant cenobite, I write for nobody, though I am insufficient unto myself. Had I an audience in mind, I would be a charlatan, and one of the moneychangers in the temple of the arts. There is no imagined public for him who would fillip the stars, although this may sound like a great brag. Finally, the making of literature is the sport of dust.

Am I hawking paradoxes? Or is this sidereal self love? Believe me, I was never concerned with egolatry, for I can think of no worse miscreant to offer my bleating pulses to than myself. Few are the Ishmaels who are willing to slave for men who are indifferent to them, but I follow Nietzsche's penultimate decision: "I no longer strive for my happiness, I only strive for my work."

After the *Sorrows* was completed, there was the query wrought of iron: What can I do with this satirical erotica? I sent it to Herbert Read, who, without any pribble prabbles, laureled it and suggested that I place it in the hands of Mr. James Laughlin, publisher of New Directions. He eventually published half of it—a chic, fifty-dollar edition of *The Sorrows of Priapus*, signed by Ben Shahn and me, as well as copies for the commoners. In the dumps, I considered the legend about Isis, who sailed in a wicker boat on the Nile in search of her mate, Osiris, who had been dismembered and thrown into that river by Set. She picked up all the pieces of his body except his genitals. How she mourned, no one can guess save a *mater dolorosa*.

Do not lament, kind and tender readers, this jubilant tract. *The Carnal Myth* is no spado, nor is *The Sorrows of Priapus*.

Well, according to the sages, the half is always better than the whole since it causes people to be dissatisfied; and is there a man more morbid than the contented churl who tells you that he is so complete that he does not even need you. But halved though I am, I shall require every one of you, now and after my demise, who need me. No other certitude have I.

One more prospect had harrowed up my spirit: I had to reread the *Sorrows* and select the quantum of chapters he desired. Books are not written, they are rewritten, and so many times that when the vision is ended, one wants to step out of it straightway. Addison and Steele were so bored with the *feuilletons* that went to the editors of the *Spectator* that either one or the other refused to make any emendations. The same is true of Balzac and Tolstoi, who could not suffer their work until it had appeared, and then they spoke of the consolation of print. I had been shackled to the *Sorrows* since 1951, beginning to study for it in New York; I continued it at Topango Canyon and Santa Monica, again taking up the *Sorrows* in Berkeley, where it rained for eight months. (I recommend horrid weather for the writer, for then he has nothing else to do but meditate.) By the time I had finished it, I fainted and fell on the floor, which reminds me of the fabled pelican, who nourishes fledglings with her own blood.

This is the story of *The Sorrows of Priapus*, and he who quits this narration less sagacious than he was before he squandered his precious hour or so upon it has been fleeced. Should a jobbernowl complain that this jocose tale is tedious, flat, and sodden, I repeat what Robert Burton, fantastical author of *The Anatomy of Melancholy*, hurled at such an abominable chuff: "If you don't like my book, go and read another."

I

THE MAJORITY of persons choose their wives with as little prudence as they eat. They see a trull with nothing else to recommend her but a pair of thighs and choice hunkers, and so smart to void their seed that they marry her at once. They imagine they can live in marvelous contentment with handsome feet and ambrosial buttocks. Most men are accredited fools shortly after they leave the womb, and these ninnies are always drunk for women. Sometimes they fall into convulsions over a piece of vermilion cloth wrapped about the bodice of a drab, not perceiving they could have just as well taken for a spouse a swath of red material, and for much less expense and trouble. The salacious zany is enticed by a petticoat or the saffron hair of the pard. These simpletons never cease to hurry after affliction, pain, and lawsuits, and if they have received a patrimony, they at once dissipate it on a chit with the mind of a goose and the avarice of Cleopatra. The harlot has a mouth of honey, warns Solomon, but the wine she gives is heavily paid for later. It is wise to remember that Livia, the procuress for Augustus, was the grandmother of Agrippina, the lupine mother of Nero.

The rabid fornicators are in a great hurry when gendering, and there are many divorces for this reason. At first they are uxorious husbands, and their wives, accustomed to such wanton and unruly attentions, later find the indifference of them insupportable. With this in mind, Aristotle advises men not to give their wives unusual pleasures. The madness for rapturous sensations has brought about countless infidelities, greed, and a plethora of thieves and effeminates. The Egyptians removed the nose of an adulteress; and this showed much wisdom, for no matter how toothsome the mouth is or how soft the haunches, Venus without a nose cannot sustain the most vehement ardor.

Every confusion comes from Eros; clothes and dyes inflame human beings, and Plato was so mindful of this that he said that boys and girls should go into the gymnasium naked as they did in Sparta. The uterus enrages the human race; the mind and the testes are similar to the twins of the Roman spouse Pliny mentions, one resembling her master, and the other the butler.

The rout blame their wives for their own faults. Euripides says: "It is to be expected that the husband of a bad wife be bad." No one can attribute his weakness or vice to another; the flaw is always in one's self, and he who is malicious or vindictive gelds his own mind and person. One can diminish himself but not the knave or the thief by an act of contumely or a fierce retaliation. It is impossible to harm another soul, good or wicked; this is the one part of man that connot be penetrated or grasped.

Poets whose works send men to brothels are themselves becrazed or in constant need of prostitutes. Men have enough to do to toil against vices without being inflamed by books. No one, except a witling, desires to be a profligate; and it is absolute insanity to drop one's seminal strength into new vessels every night. One pines because he did not take a maid who offered herself to him, and he gnashes his teeth because another has received the transitory spasms of pleasure he has refused. "If I save you, O virgin, will you thank me?" is the compunction of one character in Euripides. In later years men recall their own kind acts with boundless gratitude, but it is as impossible to remember any physical ecstasy as it is to know how Helen of Troy looked. We can only imagine, and even the great poet Homer does no more than intimate that she is beautiful.

Helen had genius, but only knew how to employ it when she had lagging, curried dugs, and long after Ilium had been cindered. As an aging matron, when her thighs and matrix were no longer sharply coveted by mortals, she was a soothsayer and knew how to alleviate the anger or sorrow of a man. A woman who can temper human anguish is a sibyl; Pythagoras thought that metaphysics wore out the heart. Our loins shake when we regard the riggish Helen who has lain in the bed of Paris, but we respect the elder wife of Menelaus more. However, it is fatuous to assume that she could no longer arouse men: Plato had a wrinkled mistress from Colophon; and whether experienced women are systolic or not, they are as lubricous as Clytemnestra. It is idle to think that men who go to older women for pleasure are dotards, and also inane to assume that wisdom is in the young and that Nestor has a doddering mind.

The cult of the body makes women *gery shrewe*, and from such females men beget fops, and dunciads. In a moment of contrition Helen calls herself a bitch. The serving maids of Penelope are, in Shakespeare's word, *brachs*.

Every one develops his vices, few water or nourish one virtue; it is for this reason hard to avoid false or true surmise; no man, when he sees the snare being prepared for him, is willing to believe that the flesh artists, the harlots of sensations, Agrippina and Poppaea, are not affectionate. Poppaea has every skill for the longest and most delirious sexual bout, and her voluptuous understanding is taken for love. She is as cold as the *phagrus*, which has a stone in its head; and when this freezes, the fish falls into a frenzy.

We suspect the odor and decay of fungus and the snail in women but seldom are clever enough to depart from any evil. Women are all our folly; few can walk away from Agrippina, Messalina, or Clytemnestra. Any of these three women has far more aptitude in venery than men. They are the spiders of the human race, and they can draw almost anybody into their webs.

Do you understand the ways of birds, brutes, and bawds? The sparrow stands erect in coition, the hen crouches, the elephant lies on her back, bears hug one another, and hedgehogs face each other. What Agrippina and Clytemnestra had not learned from the sparrow, the hen, the elephant, the bear, and the hedgehog, they acquired from the monkey, who falls into any posture to satiate his lust.

Jupiter gave the Romans seven halcyon days before the winter solstice and seven after it, which is all that flesh can tolerate. Homer says that Ulysses was a waster of cities; scarce married, he left Penelope to pillage Ilium and the beds of Calypso and Circe. Calypso is the sorceress with many girdles, and Circe the sexual snake; the offspring of Circe and Ulysses was said to be immune from the venom of the serpent. Man without the poison of the adder has no intellect, and women lacking it are unable to fold their serpentine loins about Adam. Adam paid no attention to Eve, or even noticed that she was naked, until the snake in the garden gave her the cunning to entice Adam to eat of the Tree of Knowledge, which, alas, bears the fruit of lust.

There are many legends regarding the infidelity of Penelope. She is supposed to be the mother of goatish Pan by one of the wicked suitors. It is also related that Hermes came in the shape of a goat and lay with Penelope, who gave birth to Pan. There are the tales of the poets of the Comedy, who are connoisseurs of the celestial rumps of nymphs and of beef. The later fables about Penelope show a great decline in the chastity of women. Priapus dominates Hellas, and in Caesar's Rome who, save the elders, and Catullus, remember the epithalamium that was once sung when the bride, fragrant with woodbine and marjoram and virtue, was placed in the thalmus.

Troy is sacked for Helen and ore; because Menelaus was a wittol, was it necessary to make a holocaust of mothers, sons, and daughters? For the possession of one particular womb he had to kill the honeycombed town of Asia Minor. Had he a little sense, he would have taken another wife.

Men are either enthusiastic whoremongers or warriors. Faint-hearted Menelaus was good for nothing and was as mediocre in battle as he was in Helen's arms.

The adulterer maims friends and makes of whole races a carcase to recapture the nose, the teats, the secret parts he cannot even memorize. Men fear to give their affections because they have the utmost dread of growing the horns of the wittol. The prey of the conycatcher raises some compassion; the cuckold arouses the laughter of the bulls and the noise of the timbrel. A boar without tusks will not go near the sow, and the cuckold is just as helpless; mistrust breaks his whole nature. He skulks beneath the stones and cohabits mutely without attachment.

Homer tells that Menelaus sprang from the lineage of the Asiatic voluptuary Tantalus, who was too forceless to endow Menelaus with strength. When Agamemnon went to Priam he left a bard to counsel his wife in virtue and abstinence. Agamemnon, also, had been of no more use to Clytemnestra than Menelaus was to the licentious lady of Troy. Aegisthus, the lover of Agamemnon's wife, took the poor bard out to a desert island and killed him so that he could lie with Clytemnestra without hindrance, song, or advice.

There is less trouble in the world when we are reared by streams, animals, trees, as legend says of some of the heroes of Hellenic philosophy. The river Achelous was a parent, and the epical foe of Achilles was the watery Scamander and the river Melos was said to be the father of Homer. Faustulus, the shepherd discovered the infants Remus and Romulus sucking the dugs of a wolf beneath a fig tree. He took them to his wife Laurentia to rear, but it is alleged that she was the strumpet of goatherds and was called Lupa. This fable prepares us for the woeful annals of Rome, but it is not often that the lineage of a people is available or that it is possible to learn whether a nation has sprung from a volcano, a quiet grove of poplars, or from the ribs of Numa. The most valorous men have strong animal origins, and they are the teachers of blushes and modesty.

Man became lascivious when he moulted his feathers and cast away most of his hair. He is now the most beautiful of the animals and, unfortunately, the most alluring. The ass rages for the body though its beauty is as short-lived as the fig and the pomegranate. This leads people to think that exquisite sensibility is the same as feeling; all persons love their own experiences, and those who have unusual art in scenting human skin, asphodels, or the willow are regarded as good and thoughtful.

Naked Diana awakens trembling felicity because she is almost entirely skin. So ridiculous is human desire, she is also highly esteemed because she has heavy hair on her head and but a small nest of it around her secret parts. Others will reject a woman with the hirsute legs of Esau, unless she has an opulent dowry.

Priapus is a scurrile noddy and an ignoramus, and no one can regulate his habits or predict his taste. He is as easily shared by a harpy as by a mermaid. He often prefers a jade with balding eyebrows or a goatish smell. He gathers up odors like corruption. The mother of the Scythian race was a monster, half virgin and half viper; from the buttocks upward she resembled a woman, but she had the lower parts of a serpent.

The more feeble man becomes, the more subtle are his

sexual arts. As he grows in mind, the more fierce is his desire to retain the habits of the beast. Pliny held that, the longer the world lasts, the lesser bodies shall nature produce. The weak demand exceptional orgies. The debilitated man is hard to please, and he has no palate or appetite for a Venus without rare blemishes. Human powers have been declining for many millenniums. Hector guttled away his energies when Ilium was besieged. He went from Andromache's bed straight to battle, and it may be said that it was not Helen but Andromache that destroyed Troy. Hector was an Asiatic epicure, and Andromache was abnormally big which was a reason for the long erotic revels each day before he had to face an Achilles or one of the two bulky Ajaces.

The apple and the unguents are no longer enough; a slattern excites the dandy most, or a seam of hair on the upper lip of Aphrodite, or a rank armpit. Ovid explains that Roman cosmetics came from the part of the wool where sheep sweated most. Woman now, unless she is positively mediocre and has no excessive foible or malady, will not be without a husband.

Libidinous women make the worst wives, for they are testy, and as soon as they have exhausted their husbands, they look for another one. The blood cannot boil all day long; and as wise Pythagoras's niece once said, a woman ought to cast aside her continence when she sheds her petticoats, and resume it again when she puts them on.

Everything comes in twos, good and evil, pleasure and asceticism, life and dying. Hermes is the god of eloquence, and this winged courier brings the right words to the mouth of the poet, and he also tells him when he is to die.

There is no writing, or life, or teaching that is good that is not heavily impregnated with death. Woman is two by nature; chaste Artemis is a midwife, and she assuages the hardships of parturition, but she herself has no children. Daphne preferred to be a tree rather than submit to the embraces of Apollo. Such women, provided they are not cold or glum, are sorceresses, weavers, or steadfast friends.

Hecuba remarks that no one will prefer the bed of Cassandra to the spear of Achilles, and whether she is speaking of courage or not, it has another meaning besides what Euripides gave to it. Agamemnon was puerile in taking Cassandra, for a young prophetess is an ineffectual bedpartner, and she is more likely to be thinking of a treatise on the soul or to ask whether Plato regards the earth as a cube than to be raising her haunches and employing her loins to the best advantage of her beloved.

A virtuous beauty is a plant whose first fruits are bitter, but the roots of her character are fragrant. She is similar to a plant whose power is in all parts of her rather than one. A noble woman has some wintry stone in her. It is not Plutus, greed, that gives, nor a hot drab that retains her husband, but Vesta, who guards the marriage threshold and drives the adulterer away.

Plain feeding makes for lasting, humble wedlock, and according to Dionysius of Halicarnassus, there was not a divorce in Rome for five hundred and twenty years. The first Roman to divorce his wife was Spurius Carvilius, and he was hated forever afterward for this act.

Abigail who has the understanding, carnal heart, relieves David the Psalmist rather than Adonis, and lamed Vulcan, husband of Aphrodite, is more virile and eager for her favors than a coxcomb from Crete.

It is preposterous to think that Clytemnestra killed Agamemnon in his bath to get what the weasel and the martin possess. This is the organ that mocks the mind, which dupes the man. For the heart imagines evil that the foot, the hands, and the head cannot know except by dream or accident. Those who despair of the race know that man cannot be seraphic until nature has altered his body. Maybe higher man will be a eunuch. It is a forlorn thought; and while we ponder such a future, in which we can have no share, we thank Zeus for this, who, when he lay with Alcmena, made the night three times as long. Let us weep for Tammuz; bring the first fruits and the white poplar flowers to Priapus; here is wine and oil and balsam for Phallus.

The Nile overflows when the etesian winds blow, and there are heavy rains in Ethiopia at the rising of the Dog Star; but man's desires are out of season and at odds with the little, growing seeds, the bulbs, the tubers and the up-swelling sod. There is a time for the crop of kisses, a month for borning and begetting, the season for dirges and sorrow. The wisest planter waits for all things to happen and to come to him. The patient man loves longest and best.

Myrrh, galbanum, and nard are the Shulamite and the griefs thereof. The olive, fig, and the pomegranate are Abigail, and Bathsheba of the Psalmist. Fire, air, water, earth are grass, fungus, and pride. The fruits of Jerusalem and Hellas suffer most from the worm and the caterpillar. Man is a delicate vine bruised by rain, dew, and the zephyr, which give the scab of Venus.

Jacob gave thought to his sons and considered the wolf, the adder, and the ass's colt, and then blessed the breasts and the vulva. That the suckling of a deer takes aliment from Indian paps is no matter. God bless Sarah, Hagar, Rebekah, Rachel, and Bilhah, Jacob's concubine whom Reuben trod; for sufficient unto the day are the nipples and the womb thereof.

II

MARS AND VENUS are the two pests of humanity.

Men are mad most of their lives; few live sane, fewer die so. Life is a vast solitude, and whether alone or with a wife, man is beside himself, which is to say that he is possessed. The acts of people are baffling unless we realize that their wits are disordered. Man is driven to justice by his lunacy. Otherwise, he boasts of his faults unless necessity has come to him. Primitive people are less insane than the civilized: the Scythians drank the blood of their foes after they had slain them; the cultivated man, less coherent, seldom perceives who is his adversary or his friend, and so he drinks the gore of both. The Greeks who had been pursued by the Persian Tissaphernes for hundreds of leagues across the plains of Asia imagined that, after they had sacrificed a bull, a wolf, a bear, and a ram on a shield, the Persian would not betray them.

Darius the Persian was mad when he attacked the Scythians who had no cities, mines, or arable farms. The Scythians worshipped Vesta as their first deity, which shows a pious regard for chastity. However, a fool on his nuptial night does not know whether he has culled a maidenhead or gotten the pox. The women guarding the temple dedicated to earth were required to take a draught of bull's blood to prove that they had been continent. Democritus of Abdera, seeing a young girl passing by his garden, greeted her with "Good morning, maiden." When he perceived her rushing home at dusk, he cried out, "Good evening, woman."

There is an account of two hyperborean virgins who came to Scythia with sacred knowledge wrapped in wheat straw. The Scythians carried all their laws in their heads, having no need of books. The plays of Terence are about gluttons and parasites, but the Scythians, being too poor to have either, did not require Roman comedies.

The Scythians did not care for water; the western tub is viewed as a dirty douche by the Indians. Hot baths are in many cases surreptitious profligacy. The Scythian women pounded pieces of cypress, cedar, and the incense tree upon a rough stone, which gave off an agreeable odor. Occidental man washes his face, but it looks sour and pasty.

These people had more pious burial rites than do Atlantic citizens, who inter their dead with furtive haste. They opened the belly of the dead, filled it with bruised anise seed, incense, and parsley, and sewed it up so that their last recollection of a mother or father was rustic and aromatic.

A Libyan nomad had no other property than a bowl, a sword, a ewer, and a hut made out of the stalks of the asphodels. The earliest Romans drank from the horns of oxen. Aristotle writes that the Rhodians had drinking cups composed of myrrh, rushes, saffron, balsam, and spikenard, boiled together with clay. This is elysium for those who have no part in it.

The worst calamity to a people is luxury, for Plutus is luxury which is brutal greed which leads to the deflowering of the strength, the virtues, and the dryads of a country. The Scythians lived in frugal wooden towns, abhorring the Grecian bacchanal, for they considered dissipation a woe. Barbaric nations have no spital houses, conycatchers: when a Libyan child had a fit the mother gave him the urine of a he-goat. The old primitive Christ, with an ass's head, and Jupiter, who was in part a ram, are for the poor. The meek shall inherit the earth because the avaricious, having polluted it, go in demented herds, looking everywhere for more ground, like Demeter wandering after her daughter, Persephone.

O man, take nothing from the earth, our mother, without a prayer, and be not hurried, for waiting is history, which is always seated like contemplation and Buddha.

War is an iambic rage; battle is the amour of the insane, the voluptuous entertainment of the tyrant. Despotism comes from the insatiable belly and the scrotum. Since men are at war most of their lives, Homer could hardly write about them in any other manner. Homer knew what men liked to do best, and the *Iliad* is the record of it. Conflict is the fable of man, and those who make the chronicles of the acts of Agamemnon, Achilles, Xerxes, or Alexander of Macedon are mythographers.

After Darius had conquered the Scythians, who were standing at attention in his presence, a hare ran by, and the nomads, thinking nothing of the victorious Darius, ran after the hare to catch and cook him. The Persian king was sorely vexed, because he had sacked paupers who thought more of a hare than of Darius. The asses in Darius's camp showed more generalship than he; they were so wanton that they entirely confused the horses of the Scythians when the latter, in a retaliatory skirmish, came to assault Darius's troops.

When Darius sent messengers to Greece, demanding earth and water, the Athenians cast one into a pit and the other into a well, saying, "Here are earth and water for Darius!"

At the time Darius fled from the battlefield, he escaped the pursuing hosts of Alexander because he rode a mare who was eager to return to her colt, for she had recently foaled.

The Persian rulers were examplary madmen, rarely falling into moments of good judgment. Darius, Cambyses, and even Cyrus were deranged most of their lives; Xerxes was insane all day long. Xerxes and his wife, Amestris, were poets of carnage; they are the wild parsley or water hemlock of the human race. Xerxes came to Greece with countless female bakers, concubines, eunuchs, and Indian dogs, and his army resembled an effeminate, Asiatic belly at table. This host of men dried up streams, and entire cities prepared flour and meal for many months, fattened cattle and fowl in coops and ponds, to feed his troops.

The Athenians, hearing reports of this titan stomach that was marching toward them, went to the oracle at Delphi and were informed that they would be destroyed by Xerxes.

When grief, disaster, or the jealousy of others overtake men, they are as helpless as the Romans, who, after the Tiber had washed away their houses and myriads of citizens, could do little else than consult the Sibylline Books.

Two oracles are better than one. When the Athenians saw that they were doing nothing but shaking with dread of Xerxes—and this is no condition in which to make ready for any fate—their messengers returned to the Delphian god, who delivered a more ambiguous report concerning the future of the Greek cities.

When man is in doubt regarding his soul or the strength of his character, he will labor for his destiny, which is what the Greeks did; and their triumph over Xerxes cost them less than a few hundred men.

Xerxes' army was senseless passion, but Xerxes was a dithyrambic lunatic. Enraged with the Hellespont for destroying the bridges of white flax and papyri constructed by the Phoenicians and Egyptians who were with him, he ordered that the strait be given three hundred strokes. When Xerxes was on board ship and a storm arose, he asked his pilot what could be done to prevent the vessel from sinking. After he was told that there were too many men on board, he asked the superfluous Persians to show their loyalty to their king by jumping overboard and drowning themselves. Later Xerxes gave the pilot a handsome present for saving his life but had him beheaded for diminishing the number of Persians in his army.

The Persians soon ate up Greece and were quickly afflicted with hunger and dysentery; they had no food but bark, leaves, and the boiled ropes of their beds. At war the needy Persians had behaved like demigods and the most frugal Pythagoreans, Ebionites, or Essenes. They healed their wounds with myrrh, and their table was even more bleak than that of the sages.

Xerxes was as ecstatic at home as abroad; he feared his wife Amestris more than he did the Greeks, and so committed two follies. Being a poor soldier, he was inordinately licentious, living like Silenus in the garden of Midas, where the roses were unbearably fragrant. He conceived a tormenting passion for his brother's wife. He could not seduce her, and he was unwilling to ravish her, for what exquisite reasons one cannot determine. Imagining he could draw her more closely to him through even a more intimate family connection, he arranged to have her daughter marry his son. Such a marriage would result in children, and this would bring the much-coveted mother to the palace and to his private apartment.

Venus is adroit in humbling the man who desires her, and Mercury himself is poor of tongue when Venus slips her heel out of her sandal. A philosopher may know the weather of the stars, but it will avail him nothing when Aphrodite strokes her skirt. Woman's body is her wisest mind, against which man is raving dust. At her mirror and her cosmetics, she is the poet of affectations: her pomade, stybium pot, and jewels garnish her wiles. She is almost an impeccable dissembler. Of all the brutes in the earth she is the best artist with her flesh.

The son of Xerxes married the daughter. The felicity of Xerxes was unimaginable, and his rapture was unendurable, for he immediately fell in love with the daughter, who accepted him!

In his delirium Xerxes asked his new daughter-in-law what

she wanted most. He was prepared to present her with four thousand square miles of sterile Scythian territory, the River Nile, and a thousand vineyards. She asked for nothing except the mantle Amestris had woven for him. The Persian king was dumfounded and offered her the command of an army, the revenue of ten handsome cities, and much gold. She had no intention of pouring down her lissome throat the Persian Gulf or the Nile. She had the most genuine love for him and desired only what he feared most to give her.

Xerxes gave her the mantle. When it came to the ears of Amestris that her daughter-in-law was wearing the cloak she had made for her husband, she conceived a mortal hatred for the mother of the daughter. This was a very reasonable passion: Was not the goat who conceived the kid at fault rather than the adulteress, since she could not have been troublesome had she not been born? Amestris had long since passed her jocund season, and the flesh that once had entertained Xerxes was now wrinkled. Amestris had taken fourteen children of the best Persian families and buried them alive as a holy sacrifice to the earth. She hated seedtime and all the darling, good fruits of the sun.

Once a year on the king's birthday a great festival was given, and on this occasion a monarch could not deny the petitioner whatever he desired. Amestris came to the banquet and demanded as her present the mother. Xerxes at once summoned his brother, who was married to the mother, and said, "Don't cohabit with your wife any more, but take instead my daughter," but the brother of Xerxes replied, "Sire, I like to lie with my wife," a remark which infuriated Xerxes.

Xerxes, like Zeus, had sex all over his body, and could bring forth Minerva from his head or Bacchus from his thigh. Still, he was as helpless as Zeus, who loved Troy, for gods that have genital organs are as foolish as men, and as unreliable. This the Persians knew, for they paid the highest prices for eunuchs because they said they were faithful.

It is not certain why Xerxes was anxious to save the life of his brother's wife, except that he still pined for her, since he had possessed everything else, and a tyrant can never be satisfied. Meanwhile, Amestris instructed the bodyguards of Xerxes to take the mother, cut off her breasts, ears, nose, and hands, and then return her to her husband. When the brother of Xerxes saw his wife so mutilated and slain, he went to Bactria and there raised a revolt, and for his perfidy Xerxes slew him.

At the time Cyrus came to the throne, he realized that the Persians had grown effeminate and weak through excessive gendering and feeding on whole camels. He said that a country that has delicate fruits produces delicate men rather than valiant soldiers. Understanding their error, they left the soft vineyards and the fertile plains and repaired to a hard, barren country. To be strong and rough for war, they lived like Diogenes, who was content with a barley cake and who said that the best appetizer was hunger!

*   *   *   *   *

Man is a martial animal, either riggish or bored, and only half-domesticated. Battle and gain are his religious amusements. Man casts away peace for war, for Ilium, Helen, pelf and copulation.

Epical companionship is the hymn of Ares; it is battle and strife; one must be as prepared for truth, love, or a friend, as Diomedes was ready at all times for rapine, sleeping on a hard bed with upright spears planted near enough to grasp them. Chrysostom said that the Thebans bore the marks of spears on their bodies, which had been left by the dragon's teeth Cadmus had sown. As man is a negative animal, legends and history inform us that he is seldom trustworthy except in battle. "War is the father of progress," says Heraclitus, a stygian augury.

We do not admire the wrath of Achilles, nor Ajax the dolt, nor the violence of Alexander of Macedon. The latter, however, was the perfect predacious brute. War was the orphic occupation of Alexander, one of his Muses; Minerva is the goddess of battle and wisdom. Ezekiel, Amos, Plato, Moses, and Christ teach us what man should do; Alexander informs us what he is. His disposition was a marvel among men; niter cleanses the sinner; murder purged Alexander. When he razed the city of the Getae to the ground, he paid his vows to the River Ister; the corrupt, too, speak of the angels. After slaying Clitus, one of the Hundred Companions, he kept to his tent for three days without food or drink. He had the same passion for his friend Hephaestion that Achilles showed Patroclus. When Hephaestion died, Alexander crucified the physician who attended him; and to garnish his funeral ecstasies, he made a dionysiac pyre of an entire town of innocent inhabitants. After pillaging the Ephesians, he forced them to be dutiful to the gods by giving annual tribute to Artemis.

Alexander extirpated Thebes, sparing the house of the poet Pindar. After his Bacchic siege of the Thebans, he sacrificed three boys, the same number of vestals, and three jetty rams to appease the Theban manes. He mimicked the deeds of Achilles and said his mother Olympias was the descendant of Triptolemus, son of Achilles, and he was reported to have worshipped the grave of Priam because he was the father of Hector. Alexander once ran naked around the tomb of Achilles. He paid his vows to the fifty Nereids, the most renowned of whom were Calypso, Amphitrite, and Thetis, the mother of Achilles.

Alexander was indifferent to women; Babylon, Arabia, Palestine, India, Africa were his meal. When one of the Companions spoke of the beauty of Darius's wife, Alexander said he had no desire to see her. Agamemnon sacrificed his daughter, Iphigenia, to appease Diana, showing the little concern he had for the fruit of the womb. Men may waste away for the favors of women, which at least is a logical greed, but no one can fill his gullet with several seas and continents or has the human strength to walk once around a domain that includes Asia and Europe. This is cold venery, and the most difficult to understand. If a man drinks two or three gallons of wine, beer, or ordinary water, he is a sloven bladder. What can any mortal do with seven oceans? This greed is as droll as the junk cony of Patagonia, at the door of whose burrow lies a breccia of bones, dung, shells, or a clock or skewer he has pilfered from a neighboring house.

Every man who cannot be Aristotle would like to be Alexander of Macedon. He destroyed the oldest cities in the earth, and ravaged annals precious to sane mortals. Tyre, meaning the "rock," *tsor*, in Hebrew, he overthrew, and ransacked Phoenicia which comes from the Greek word *phoinix*, or palm tree. The Macedonian king seized Cyprus, a Tyrian colony of Hittites, who furnished King Solomon with numerous wives. The Tyrians who took refuge in the temple of Hercules he pardoned, because he regarded himself as a descendant of that hero. Thirty thousand of these Canaanites, mostly women and children, were sold into slavery.

The *Iliad* he knew by heart, and held games in honor of the Muses. Alexander prized friendship, calling his best generals the Hundred Companions. In a dream he saw a swallow perched upon his head, and at once suspected that the Hundred Friends were conspiring to kill him. His soothsayer, Aristander the Temisian, quieted him by telling him that the swallow is a loquacious bird and signified an informer who would disclose the plot against him. A familiar of every crime, he believed that each person had his own vices.

Man is unstable all the days of his life; most of his acts are contrary to his interests. He is the spoiler of his own good fortune because he cannot wait for it. He relies either upon everybody or on no one. The fool has confidence in all people; the knave trusts himself. He seldom knows when he is cuckolded or who is his conycatcher.

The best commonwealth is one in which every citizen governs himself well. Alexander was a saturnalian Spartan. He had seizures of self-abnegation. When the daughters of Darius were his captives, he did not touch them; going through the desert, he refused water because his soldiers had none; at the same time he rode through the burning sands playing a flute and clothed in the habit of Dionysus. Though he worshipped Bacchus, he destroyed Thebes, which was sacred to that god. On Mount Meros, named for Zeus's thigh, in which Bacchus grew, Alexander and his Macedonians celebrated the drunken Revelry for ten days. Obviously he disciplined himself when he had the appetite for it, particularly after he had destroyed twenty cities or had killed a friend. He could not tolerate any opposition and hanged two thousand Tyrians by the seashore for no other cause except that he was unable to capture that formidable rock in the sea as quickly as he had expected. The kite, owl, and sea pie are antagonists to the raven, but there is no one who hates one man so much as another does.

Gaza fell down before him, and the infant and the mother were driven into bondage. He cut holes into the feet of Batis, the brave defender of Gaza, and put brazen rings through them, after which he dragged Batis behind his chariot in imitation of Achilles, who had done this with the corpse of Hector. At Memphis he bowed down to Apis, who had never shown much interest in him. He had also taken possession of the city of Priapus, but it was a bootless spoil. It may be that he gave grave offense to Bacchus, in whose nocturnal ceremony the women hold the phalloi aloft, because he lacked this kind of energy. Alexander of Macedon had the body of Adonis, but this was a god whom the Pythagoreans and the Greek poets did not consider very potent. Venus was supposed to show Adonis her favors, but she is not a wise goddess.

Alexander kept three hundred and sixty-five concubines, who followed his army, because it was a Persian custom. He had adopted the livery of Darius, wearing the purple vest, loose scarlet trousers, and a robe of regal hue. He plundered Babylon, Susa, Egypt, Ecbatana, the empire of the Indies, to garb himself in the colors of the goose.

Alexander laid waste to a great part of his army to smell the myrrh trees and roots of nard in the country of the Ichthyophagi, or the fish-eating Gadrosians. He had the most poignant desire to overcome this impoverished land, where the inhabitants lived in hovels made of mussel shells and roofed with the backbones of fishes. The principal food of these beggars was fish, which he forbade them to eat since this is not regarded as a heroical diet in the *Iliad*. Homer, according to ancient writers, thought the fish in the Hellespont was poor for eating. But then, Alexander's Greek was clumsy.

The raven in Greenland feeds on the offals of seals, and its meat is disgusting; the skin of Alexander was as fragrant as Syrian spices. Babylonian fields were covered with frankincense; cinnamon was torn from shrubs, and the wild meadows produced spikenard. Grief, battles, and murder were Homeric rituals and aromatic plants for Alexander; at the time of the vintage thrushes, glutted with nutmegs, fall down to the ground drunk. Alexander, as intoxicated as a thrush, swollen with nutmegs, ached to seize indignent Mount Meros, which had furnished Dionysus with ivy; he overcame savage Mount Caucasus, where asafoetida, which delights goats, was abundant and terebinths grew on the barren flanks. Belus, the deity of Babylon, had predicted that he would meet his fate in that land, but Alexander, plucking his words from Euripides, answered, "The best prophet is he who guesses well."

Alexander was as crapulous as our passions. He burnt the palace at Persepolis because Thais the harlot urged him to do it. Parmenio, one of the Companions, asked him why he was destroying his own property. The Uxians, impecunious nomads, fell before his javelins. Who goes to war with poverty or loots Lazarus for his gold? It is an absolute delusion to go out into the world with an immense, rich army to pillage gravel.

Had Alexander of Macedon moral faculties, Seneca would have been his poor counterpart. The moral behavior of the alpine daw is different from that of the carrion crow; the two are almost alike, the former having a smaller bill and a sniveling cry. If we understood the anatomy of character as much as the ornithologist knows the sundry species of birds, it would be possible to distinguish between Peter and Judas. Were the tail of the magpie shorter and were there no white in his plumage, he would be a crow. The conduct of the feathered tribes can be ascribed to the craw, the talons, and how they employ their mandibles. Pascal said that the history of the ancient world was the result of the shape of Cleopatra's nose.

The jay, raven, crow, and magpie are robbers, having the disposition of Sisyphus and Alexander. The jay could be taken for a frugivorous Essene did he not prey upon the young of other birds. The nutcracker closely resembles the jay, but he has a different bill, and he dwells in the mountains and is content with the kernels of pine tops. The abode of birds, whether they are mountain dwellers, or love glades, or are pernicious, depends upon the contour of their chaps, rumps, and the color of their plumage.

Alexander was as vehement as the jay, and as crafty as the magpie. The jay, unable to fill his gullet with all the filberts, chestnuts, and sorbs he craves, buries what he cannot eat. The acorns which he has hidden, but cannot remember where, spring up as oaks. The jay is a wastrel, and at times is so violent that he gets his head entangled between two branches and hangs himself. One observer saw a bird tied to a tree who endeavored to peck a morsel, but each time a magpie swept the food away with his tail. The magpie prattles as much as Socrates, but is malicious.

Socrates and Paul, who had doughty bodies and amorous blood, but powerfully tethered, were testy; knew we more of their physical structure, we might better understand how to distinguish between the owls of Judea and Attica. Our knowledge of the anatomy of Alexander is as meager. He marvelled at all origins and sailed down the Hydaspes to the great sea looking for the source of the Nile. Mammals and birds astonished him. When Bucephalus disappeared, he threatened to extirpate the whole Scythian nation if his horse were not returned. He imposed a severe penalty upon anybody who slew the peacock of India. He killed thousands of Indians, but this did not delight him as much as did the elephants he found pasturing near the river Indus.

Stony, bare places gemmed his intellect. He took possession of a rock inhabited by the barbaric Sogdianians, and seized a sterile site known as the rock of Chorienes. There was a legend that Hercules had been unable to capture the rock called Aornus. Alexander overcame this massy stone. Had he an ominous dream, or did some one fall ill, such as Coenus, his friend, he poured out libations to the river gods who wear fillets of sedge and who were known as Nereus and Amphitrite; this was metaphysics as well as murder.

When Alexander lay in his tent groaning because he had murdered Clitus, Anaxarchus told him he was as just as his father Zeus. Anaxarchus had given offense to two deities: justice, which is philosophy, and the bastard Muses, for he was a poetaster. Many escape the one vengeance of the Muses (otherwise how could so many bad writers flourish?), but none can avoid the wrath of justice. Later, Anaxarchus offended Niocreon, king of Cyprus, who had him pounded to death in a mortar.

When Hephaestion died, Alexander had all the manes of the mules and horses shorn, and cut his own hair, because this was the way in which Achilles mourned over the corpse of Patroclus. The Cosseans he burnt alive, offering them as a funeral pyre to the shades of Hephaestion. Slaughtering thousands of Persians, he tortured the Magians, who had not protected the tomb of Cyrus, son of Cambyses. Self-abnegation was also one of his frenzied rites, when an Indian gymnosophist, failing in health, had resolved to die, he prepared the faggots for him, and as the Indian philosopher Calanus lay down in this funeral bed of fire, the Macedonian soldiers uttered the war cry, trumpets were sounded, and the elephants snorted.

After a drunken revel, Alexander plunged into the Tigris, and grew a fever; he endeavored to cure the fatal drowsiness by baths, swimming, offering sacrifices to the gods, and more drinking bouts. Seven of the Companions, seeing Alexander's life ebb away, slept in the temple of Serapis, entreating that deity for help. Ares was his god, and not Apis, Busiris, or Mnevis, for the bull in the Serapeum was not concerned with his destiny.

Who wears the garments that smell of myrrh, aloes, and cassia gives little thought to his last hour. We either drink up our force or meditate upon the banks of Cocytus. Either we live for our end, or we are tempted. It is noble, says Pascal, to be weary and worn out by the vain pursuit of the true and the good. All other fatigue is lust and the tears of the dotard.

When Alexander died, rumor girdled the earth. There was a report that Aristotle, who had been his tutor, had sent a poison, sealed in the hoof of a mule, which had brought an end to the Macedonian conqueror. The bones were scarce cold before the Companions killed each other; Olympias, his mother, was assassinated; Roxana and her issue by

Alexander were murdered; another widow and son, Barsine and Hercules, were destroyed.

Alexander sacked the greater part of the globe for the spices of the Moluccas, pelf, destruction of whole nations, reverently titled history, which is the idolatry of power, gore, and war.

III

SOCRATES advised men not to involve themselves in useless inquiries about how the world was produced. Cosmology is a marvelous sickness of the intellect, and geography is her handmaiden. Strabo showed the greatest veneration for Homer's knowledge of rivers, seas, and lands. The sea is deceitful, as Homer and Virgil teach, and men who spend their time like Thales, the metaphysician of water, or as Anaxagoras musing upon the Cosmos have marine dispositions, and could they be fathomed one would find that the images and ideas at their watery bottom were of the shape of prehistoric fish or of primeval ocean substance.

Pelagic men smell of foam, kelp, bridle weed; their ideas and handshake come from sea olives and sea thyme, which sprout stones in the gulf. The sole labor of the water mind is to find out what is primal. Salt is older than the Deluge, and the meditative man is brackish. Cranes from Scythia fly each year to the salty bogs; the Nile, one of the first rivers in the world, begins in the saline marshes.

Human faculties have their summer solstice and their February dirges; the mind is neither water, shell, skin, nor fire. It is good and then evil, savage and domestic. Austere minds produce wormwood, which thrives in cold regions; the olive on wintry mountains is barren. The ocean intellect has original force; the sea oak grows on stones and oyster shells but has no roots, and is without affections. Seaweed tangles the Pillars of Hercules, where the swag-bellied tunny eats Mediterranean acorns. In the beginning were the great waters and fuci, and after that came mud, the masts, and the fat, sun-loving tunny.

Oceanic seers are mammoths of inhuman wisdom, riverine savants come second; earthy thinkers are social; of fire are the phoenix and sphinx wrought. Heraclitus remarks that a dry soul is the wisest.

Socrates was a rigid Spartan, enduring privations to which no Athenian slave would submit, but his frugal habits were the result of reflection. Socrates was boastful, even a quibbler, as Timon said, and sensual. Balded by lechery, or seeming so, Socrates is dear to our bawdy blood. Plato was a charming poet when he has the knavish but clever Alcibiades portray Socrates as a Silenus in a statuary shop, which when opened up reveals a golden deity.

The life of Socrates is a lesson to the soul because he had every human defect, but unlike the many he was himself the mastiff, Cerberus, guarding the gates of his own hell, where our sins roam without heads of substance. Philosophy is the watchdog of man and is what Plato, Socrates, and Cicero meant when they said that this was the study of death and that Charon is the boatman of the ontological thinker.

When Socrates came to a summer ground strewn with grass and a plane tree, he thought such a place was sacred to Achelous and the Nymphs. Before leaving the tranquil spot, he prayed to Pan, entreating that rustic divinity to unite the inward soul with his exterior nature.

Once Socrates asked one of his sons, Lemprocles, whether it was worse to be hurt by a beast than by the kicks and biting of his mother. Not without boorish appetite, he regarded every exceptional outburst, whether it was anger, pleasure, avarice, or overeating, as forms of violence and disorder. He is said to have shown only one face. Aristippus, the Cynic, thought pleasure the greatest good and pain the greatest evil. Anthisthenes, a pupil of Socrates, asserted that he would rather go mad than feel pleasure. Socrates abhorred whatever unduly aroused him. When Critias the Tyrant was among the company of many of his hearers, Socrates told Critias that all he cared to do was to rub upon Euthydemus as swine scrape themselves against stones.

Socrates gave Aspasia amorous instructions; he told her how to exact the utmost gratulation from coition. This is the hot teaching, perhaps, of Pluto's and Xenophon's droll in the Agora. For he went barefoot in the snow, and endured the most sparse eating.

That he lay with Aspasia or was sorely tempted by Alcibiades is also, we suspect, apocryphal.

Neither Meletus nor Anytus, the accusers of Socrates, ever

said that he traduced boys or was a concupiscent teacher. There is the story related by Diogenes Laertius that, after Socrates took the hemlock, Meletus was given the death sentence and that the Athenians closed the Palaestra and gymnasia, and no one would go to drink at the same public fountains with the former treachers of Socrates. This is probably apocryphal because races of people are not penitent, and when they erect a brazen statue to a man they have killed, they pretend that the honored dead sage was never ridiculed, or banished, or put to death by them. A statue is a wily subterfuge, and a concealment of a truth, and few can look through the bronze to grasp the real occurrence or the man it hides.

The talker is the most trustworthy of men, for though he may often be a bore, he is not likely to be a deceiver. Anthisthenes remarked that his greatest luxury was his leisure, which he employed to be with Socrates. When Zeno arrived in Athens, he went to a bookseller who was reading aloud Xenophon's *Memorabilia*, on Socrates, and, learning that such an extraordinary man had lived in Athens, decided at once to settle there. Socrates never went to the Agora until he thought it was full of people who would hear him. When he was rebuked for saying the same thing over and over again, he answered that, if it were true, he would never tire of repeating it. It is no exceptional grace for a man whose tongue is generally shut to govern it. We would commend a Lacedaemonian for speaking, or laughing, or shaking hands, for by doing so he would be exercising his will. Were Diogenes to hold his tongue, we should praise him for his modesty. A man without appetite cannot be called virtuous because he does not rule desires that never molest him. But the gossipy tongue is an asp, for in one way or another, and often without forethought, it stings.

Babbling is as wanton as the salacious sparrow, who, according to Aristotle, is very short-lived because it cohabits excessively. But it is not the worst of faults, for no man who is garrulous conceals his meanest purposes, whereas it is hard to know whether it is the pard or the fox in the taciturn nature that is lying in wait to spoil men of their wives, property, or composure.

Plato was concerned with justice, ideal conduct, and the government of human passions, and that is what politics or any good commonwealth is about; tyranny is insolence, intractable conceit, greed, and the despisal of saying plain things simply. As Euripides says, not in obscurity but in plainness is wisdom.

There is little or no homage to Aphrodite in the *Laws*, and it is doubtful that Plato was worried about the cessation of his carnal appetites; and if he was at odd moments stung by the sight of an undergarment of one of the flute girls he introduces into the *Symposium*, he either wrote another dialogue or went to the nearby cemetery, which was then the haunt of the Athenian prostitutes, and rid himself of such a plague as quickly as possible. The life of Plato is as much of an enigma as the Beatrice of Dante, who placed the sacred amorists in the Seraphic Circle in his Paradise.

Aristotle had lubricious inclinations, for he investigated the sexual inclinations of sea animals and went to much trouble in finding out whether one fish is given to buggery at the rising of Arcturus or a mullet is best to eat when pregnant. It is not how many profligate aches a man has but with what hardihood he withstands them that draws us to him. Everybody with a warm stomach hears the sirens, and some stuff their ears with books as Odysseus sealed the ears of his sailors with wax.

Plato received all his thoughts from Apollo, the healer, and his son Asclepius and the goddess Artemis, whose name is derived from sound health. She is the most continent of the deities. Aristotle, the great pupil of Plato, was not so temperate as his master. He had all the defects of a poet, often going about in the loud garb of Bacchus and wearing rings. He was so enamored of the concubine of a tyrant that, when the latter permitted him to marry her, he offered a sacrifice. He died at sixty-three, which is a short life for a metaphysician.

We must be on guard against Aeschylus, one of the wisest of seers, because he was a drunkard; when he was a youth, he was once looking at a grapevine until he fell asleep and saw Dionysus, who told him to write tragedies. A philosopher is similar to the oak that bears acorns at the summit and bees in the middle, as Hesiod writes, for the thoughts are the top of a man and are the best fruits of his days, and if he obeys what is highest in him, his nature will flow honey. Xenocrates was said to have had such a severe face that Plato continually told him to pray to the Graces.

A grum man is hard to endure; Demosthenes had a crabbed brow, and he had a disposition that was more suitable locked up in a closet than for sociable purposes. Without strength it is almost impossible to be genial. Aristophanes says that the Athenians did not like hard and sour poets, and let us not set aside the venereal fruits of Helios or the olive that is nourished by Selene, for he who dishonors the sun or the moon and their children the grape, the pomegranate, and the olive is wicked.

The greatest wits, says Aristotle, mentioning Socrates,

Plato, and Hercules, were melancholy, but not dour. Melancholia is a disease which tires the blood. Aristotle thought that happiness is energy, but few are content to be free of these waters and winds which, according to Plato, were later called catarrh and flatulence. The wrath of Achilles we know; and one may hide until his anger is passed, or absent oneself from his person for a month or so, going to the salt depths of the Aegean sea, for brine is a marvelous simple and the dearest of cures to the heart that has been bruised by the ire or indelicacy of a friend.

Sages lose the young blush of Diana or Hippolytus but retain their faculties until death. Hippias had a most acute memory until one hundred and eight, when he died. There is no tale regarding the dotage of Plato, and though the *Laws* are void of those animal images that are known as Pan, the Satyrs, and Silenus, there is severe sagacity in this last song, his senilia, the fabled dirge of the dying swan.

The mind ages or is as deciduous as the tree which sheds its old leaves and is rejuvenated after its sere boughs are broken. The wise sit upon the ground; grapes and the gourd mature when they are clothed in dust.

At sixty one should relinquish pleasure; at fifty, prepare for abstinence or else be ready, as Plato says, to educate his diseases. Aristotle thought that reading was the viaticum of old age, and books are a far more lasting delight than the bed of Helen for whom the Trojans and Greeks became paupers. Xenocrates, one of the scholarchs of the Academy after Plato's death, was abstinent if not ascetic; when Phryne the courtesan crept into his bed with him, she had nothing to say afterward that could add to her rumored abilities.

Dionysius of Heraclea gave a banquet to his sycophants,

and there were many female dancers present, but when the most edible girl approached him, he turned to one of his pickthank friends with the following words: "You take her, I am no longer able." This is a grievous hardship, and the wise so suffer, too, though they cannot derive much satisfaction from such illogical grief. One of the wittiest hetaerae of Athens said that philosophers and poets also knocked on her door.

Ambition kills the rout and utterly ossifies the old, and as Euripides asserts, it is the worst of all the gods. Men with nothing in their heads but the desire for longevity and gain show years which fruit spite and usury. These people never toil for a single truth. God showed Solomon the highest favor because he asked for understanding rather than a long life. Solon reproached Mimnermus, the poet, who said that sixty years was enough for any man, but he was very bored and had already worn out his genitals. Solon wanted to live to eighty, which is about as long as the life of a cocoa tree; and oaks and whales are more long-lived than Xenophanes or Hipparchus, but the former are far more patient and quiet than Mimnermus. Who would not rather be leviathan than Job? There are tribes among the people of India who eat rice loaves, dwell in soft ground nourished by warm winds, and live to be one hundred and fifty years old. This, at least, is what the ancient geographers assert, though some are fabulists.

Few, young or old, struggle to be Solon or Pittacus or Bion. It requires more bravery to overcome the weariness and lassitude of old age than to go into the battlefield. Generally, the aged have a bedlam mind and are no more than wizened or bulky matter, without thought of the universe and of the beginnings of man. When one ceases to wonder, one has perished or, worse, decayed. "Wonder is the beginning of philosophy." said Plato.

The multitude are content to achieve seventy-five or eighty years without acquiring ruth or valorous conceptions. All they have to show for a toothless mouth or wrinkles is money and a debris of household possessions. What is abominable in aging men is not their ague, their cold, shaking blood, but their indifference to learning; they know nothing about Sirius, the winds, mountain laurel, or when vetch should be planted. A medieval author has written: Abishag the Shunammite alone kept the old David warm, since the love of wisdom does not desert its lover even when the body grows feeble. We hear with much desolation the waning amorist of the *Sonnets* and lament the many lustra that lie upon Euripides, who was said to have lived alone in a cave overlooking the sea at Salamis.

It is balm to decaying blood to learn that the courtesan Phoenix came to the bed of decrepit Nestor, but it is inane to sigh for the strength of a runner at the time when one should be a philosopher. Cicero mentions Milo of Crotona, who, while observing prize fighters at their exercises, shed tears over his own dead arms instead of going into similar mourning for his head. The ignorant always want to be boys; Proclus of Naucratis became the partner in the pastimes of his sottish son, who was dissipating the patrimony breeding fighting cocks, quails, puppies, and horses, and imagined that he was a spruce blade when he was only as porcine as his young son. There is more nonage among the youth than in the old in years.

Curried flesh is testy and covets what is lost, the gross, harsh tufts of hair of the hyena or the complexion of the naiads. This is not the time when Lais of Corinth would take a poet's wisdom instead of his obols for pay or Aspasia would lie with Socrates though he had not a pair of shoes on his feet. Men fear to wax mouldy as much as they shake at the thought of the ditch of Tartarus. Few care for the repose of Aeschylus, who had a tough, hairless cranium which only a rock dropped by an eagle could break. Euripides, too, moans: "Youth is ever sweet to me, old age lieth heavier than Etna."

The aged, without minds, are seasoned in falsehoods and petrified by greed, and habit has lain in their acid, trade skins so long they are incapable of rousing their faculties for any intellectual conflict whatsoever. They abhor difficult or abstract ideas, and when they hear of a chivalric conception, they are baneful Hecubas, swearing at a good thought as though she were a fury garlanded with blood and serpents. It is a perversion of the will to detest erudition.

Not many men in their middle life make new attachments; they spend most of their thoughts wailing by the walls of Jerusalem for Tammuz, which is a lamentation for their laggard tail. Shakespeare sorrowed more for his declining phallus and the filberts of groveling Caliban than he did for Ariel. In one of the tragedies of King Richard he has written: "How strange it is that desire outlasts performance."

There is no bile that so sings as in wasted and dissolute flesh; Tiberius, stale with murder, was in his seventies a Libertine, and he had more energy and genius for malice when the worms were impatient for his purulent body than when he was young, because he knew so much more. Old men have rotten, broken dreams, which are omens of their end and the foul labor of their suns and moons. How our dreams persecute us when our appetites are reechy and bloated!

IV

MAN DREADS that he may become a dotard, and that his soul may be rifled of the passions of Gethsemane. Scholars relinquish their vigor and harm their intestines to find out that the whelk has the trumpet of a triton or that dolphins couple rubbing their bellies together. There is no parturition without agony; the ova of the fish *Belone* cannot get out of her stomach except by bursting it.

The philosopher increases his knowledge as he rots; there is a sort of wolf spider who impairs her womb to furnish the material for warp threads. How noble it is to decay growing wise; oysters are generated in scummy foam around ships that have been moored a long time.

Most men close to their demise are gross sumpter-asses of business; the valiant die myriads of times, and after the reflective faculties have accomplished their work, they grow trite and fall into dotage. Bees, almost extinct, are restored to life by covering them with ox paunches and mud; the body of a horse can bring a wasp back to life. When the hides of seals are flayed and stripped from their bodies, they comprehend the tides. How sentient are the dead, and of what incalculable value is a corpse to the universe!

Melancholy or distempered elephants tear up grass, which refreshes the soul far more than the pellets of Aesculapius, which makes cowards of whole races. It is good to die casting up grass toward heaven, and he who is wise will accept his fate with the anger of a pachyderm, for it is best to die in battle. Not until we translate the death of one man into an exact quantum of energy of the universe can we be philosophers.

Since there is development instead of progress, why should we be astonished that we are of less use to clay, the bole, or to the turf than are willows or oaks, which can be converted into stone or sardonyx? Not far from the city of Coburg was a whole forest of agate. Either we are stone, or we are decayed wood which may never be transfigured into agate. It is idle and insane to complain against nature.

Strife and confusion haunt men until their death. The Greeks paid homage to a god of insolence; they brought votive offerings to Ceres, fear, and Eros. The Syrians on the Orontes showed the utmost veneration for an image of Fortune which Eutychides the sculptor had made for them. The earth has no need for the forceless; Acheron, the river of the dead, nurses white poplars, which Homer calls *Acherois*, for death is an absolute energy. The robber

Sisyphus is useful to destiny when dead, for he never ceases pushing the rock up to the mountainous peaks though it rolls down every time.

The season for sorrow, funerals, and the stubble in the wind is as regular as the time for nidification. One can count upon two to three hundred hogsheads of melancholia and waste every year before the Dog Star rises. What men ask for they harvest, for otherwise how could there be wars, ruin, and hatred? When men ate leaves and grass, they wept for the acorns of the *phlegos* oak. Then Pelasgus, the first king of Arcadia, gave them huts and pigskin shirts to protect them against rains and bogs, but mischance crept into their hovels and blouses; each one who prays to Zeus for gold, more acres, his neighbor's wife, is miserable enough to have his petition granted.

All is vanity and a striving after wind, and man has no profit of his labor except in his will. Lineage is our nemesis, foretelling our shames and how we shall go to the cerecloth. There is more bear's-foot in one brood than in another; bilberries settle on dry hillocks; toothwort sprouts beneath the hazel. What virtue is there in the crocus, which flowers in hard weather?

Olympias, mother of Alexander of Macedon, killed her husband and dragged his concubine Cleopatra and her infant son over a bronze vessel filled with fire, and Alexander himself slew ten thousand cities for no other cause but that his sire was Philip and that he was cribbed nine months in the belly of Olympias.

Have all the canticles, the thousands of poems, and the triremes that sang upon the rivers as swans betrayed us? Does knowledge make us base and killers? Cain was sent into the wilderness of Nod because he slew Abel, but each who sorrows in the solitary forests has killed one who has called him brother.

Stones are for patience, but dust is in diverse places gathering rage and derision. Expired mountains suckle marble pillars; diorite is steadfast and starves the jackal. All the unguents of Astarte do not confuse Theban limestone; gall and the palmer worm cannot be mummified, and blood is no tablet for oaths. The corridors of the pyramids are dry of tears. Wicked Cheops in his tomb is a psalm; all else is rheum and water.

Lineage thrives beneath the limestone hills; the Nubian rock is the tablet of Cush. The kings of Sidon quarried their tombs in Egypt, and the steatite scarab remembers the Hyksos prince. Remembrance is petrified in rocks and stelae; angels are hieroglyphs cut into basalt ranges. Rains breed the wanton lizard and dissolve filial love; moisture is the substance of the spider. Sun and sphinx strike the maggot.

All annals are writ in equal dust. Adages are the worms in the sarcophagus; sin and love are mathematic in the tomb. Trees sicken, and dying flowers offend, though asphodels remain the same in the meads of the dead. What lives is sin and dross save it die, for there is no hurt in the winding sheets. Death attracts the valorous mind which is possessed by Atropos, who sends him to his end. The noblest heart perishes when it disburdens its destiny. The thinker lives solely to die: this is what Pascal calls the automatic need to finish: Abba, Abba, it is finished.

Quarry the blood as old debris and mound, for rubble and brick hide Rehoboth and Akkad, and ruin is the false morsel of fear and the grub. A body laden with Arabic mumia is a cure for our sloven days of shame and Sodom.

Can the shroud of Thothmes betray the maggot? Will the peristyle cower before Scythian Vulturnus? The pectoral set in the skeletal breast is obsidian, and papyrus is the vegetable raiment of queen Hentmehit; a senile column at Persepolis is the eagle's perch, while the parched gazelle sleeps on pylons in the dunes. Desert and skull prove the tooth of doubt; blood is king of waste, but relic and chagrin are sayings and lore.

Sepulchers are the archives of knowledge; they know most whose burial rites arouse awe. The ant inters the dead, and locusts, driven in great shoals by warm winds, expire with felicity in the marshes which were the abodes of the great Assyrian kings. The grave of Daniel lies at Shus. Nebbi Younis is the tomb of the prophet Jonah; may rocks shield him from his foe, the palmer worm. At Abydos the head of Osiris lies alone. Fence in the remains of Zephaniah with the sherd of Nineveh; the lamentation of Jeremiah is pyrite, may his tomb in Samaria never have a seam. Adam lies beneath the water meadows of Damascus. Oxhead is the cemetery of Alexander's charger; opposite the prison where Joseph deciphered the dreams of Pharaoh's baker and cupbearer was a vast graveyard of horses. Cato died in Utica, which is close by the greater Syrtis, where the lotus-eaters dwelt. We avoid being Cato by as short a distance as the gulf of the Lotophagi is from Utica.

Hew the slab fresh with grief from the mountain; the cave of Machpelah will keep Abraham entire. Lend not holy Isaac to the usurious worm. Oil of cedar protects the haunches of Phut; the body of Peter was laden with honey though the ink of Hermes was steeped in galls. Cyrus is a sage in his valley grave; noble and vain are the skulls of David and Isaiah. The sepulchres of Esther and Mordecai heal Ecbatna. Give a prayer for the detritus of deceased Heliopolis that contained the feet of Asenath, Joseph's bride. What sacral rubble holds the tunic of Moses? Is there yet a jamb or lintel Plato touched?

The jackal has no respect for the winding sheet, but all knowledge is in the tomb. The Andes is a necropolis of the mastodon, the monkey, and the jaguar, and there lies prehistoric man. The burial urn expels the mad Erinyes; papyrus does not moulder in the mummy pit, for barley and corn seed grow fat by dead Pharaohs. A dried pomegranate is as entire as the body of the prophet Samuel.

The earth is millions of years old, but it has not lost its wit or mind or virtue, for everything can be found in the ground. What man regards as recondite Sophia is the discovery of a humble seed, the use of an herb, or of an ass's skin. Empedokles blew up ass's bladders to catch the etesian gales.

Sun and moon are potsherds in the Valley of the Tombs; Rā and ancient Isis sleep among papyrus flowers. Apostle Thomas is interred in Edessa; may the smallest cumin seed cover his affection. King Tchesser is now a litter of Egyptian glyphs, for he hewed his woe in a channel of rock. Buttress all mortal works in calcareous stone, for even vilest Cambyses is an admonitory inscription. Granite sustains Baalpeor and the winged bull of Ashur. The rocks of Hetnub are steadfast sons. To betray is nature; fealty is in the grave. Keep the bones and boasts of Nimrod in gypsum; ignorance pours out the strength of awe. The honey of Babylon succors Alexander; the cerecloth of Amenhotep is the tunic of Osiris. Where are the remains of Magog and the river Goshen? The burial sites at Memphis can never be filled.

Steep the body of Jacob in mountain natron; Lazarus is moldy without the nard and drugs of Gaza; bitumen preserve the skeleton of Adam; cassia and myrrh guard the father's knees. Osiris is prudent in a hundred sacred tombs. Sorrow for the dead is an olden skill. The ancient gods taught Anubis embalming, and Hermes' sandals are shod by cobblers in Orcus; heed no sighs except the epitaph of stone. A thousand slabs are more prophetic than Tiresias, and the Holy Ghost can be contained in Adam's dust.

It is unreasonable to labor for posterity, and woeful to die, but natural; to do nothing is pernicious grief. Man works to remember, and a frugal headstone has more nature in it than a cenotaph.

There is rank superstition in Egypt's *Book of the Dead* and the worship of the cat, the dog, and the beetle and crocodile. Much of the ritual of the dead of ancient Egypt is a book of the dog, and Anubis, the great god, had this beast's head. At Mendes the goat was deified, and at Leontopolis the lion received duck, veal, honey, and groats, and all this is art and raging passion.

A remnant of the Cuthites journeyed to Iberia and built beacons or lighthouses of hewn rock which had one eye and were called Cyclopes. Cyclops is the progeny of Ham.

The cat is very dear to Ham, and the pyramids are abstract stone and marble desert cats. The Egyptians are a cat people, and the art of mummifying the deceased body is a feline art. The Egyptians despised shepherds, and Jacob's sons feared to tell Pharaoh that they were tenders of cattle. Wherever the heifer is scorned, the cat is holy; and where kine are sacral animals, as in the Vedic hymns and in Judaic law, the mouse, the kite, the eagle, and the cat are unclean.

When a dog died in the house of an Egyptian, he mourned and cast away all of his grain.

Ham was the first painter, for he cared more for his own image than for anybody. In ancient Israel Ham is an idol maker, and in Egypt Cush is an architect, and in Greek civilization Ham is called Narcissus. The greatest iniquity of Narcissus the artist is that he paints himself all day long; his canvases or stone idols are feminine toilet; for the ideal of Narcissus is the lavatory, the mirror, and the waste pipes which are known as esthetics. Ham, Cush, and Narcissus were the first plumbers. Narcissus makes the most intricate abstract drawings of cubes, triangles, and lozenges, which are nothing else but surrealist porcelain latrines; these are the idyllic canals for ordure in his intellect. He is a human bowel hater, and he is coprophagous, for he eats with his mind what the prophet Ezekiel in his zeal for fallen Israel would not. There has never been human excrement in the imagination of the Prophet. Ezekiel, to do penance for the sins of Israel, takes into his mind visions of cow ordure instead of human offal. A king in India always kept an ox at his side.

THE COST OF KNOWLEDGE is dear; the arts have not made men less vain than Absalom, nor less stupid than the Emperor Claudius, who added three letters to the Roman alphabet. One author of remote times declared that a good man is at one time good and at another bad, but he who fawns upon the Muses is more difficult to grasp than Proteus.

Though man is the only beast that can write, he has small reason to be proud of it. When he utters something that is wise it is nothing that the river horse does not know, and most of his creations are the result of accident. His celebrated songs fall out by chance and were not even known to him before he set them into meter. Poems are like worms, which, Aristotle says, come from snow that has lain a long time or originate in the dung of oxen and asses.

He who does not distrust art does not comprehend philosophy; but he who really cares for metaphysics loves Artemis, Apollo, and Endymion more than Pan. Apollo gave votive offerings to Dionysus before he followed Cybele in her wanderings to the blessed hyperborean's land. The vine is tender when man piously goes out to seek the earth. As long as the lamp of Pallas Minerva is filled and its flame never ceases to glow, man can pay homage to stones, stocks, and beasts. In Egypt a massebah was polished by the kisses of worshippers.

Neither Sparta nor Athens can be our mentor. The former produced no art, which made the Lacedaemonian so dour that it was a prodigy to see a Spartan smile. It takes a great deal of intelligence or naïve affection to smile well; neither Iago nor Polonius can do it; a good, honest laugh is a birthright, which the shrewd practice and the mediocre are unable to wear. Homer says that the Athenians were a dark-eyed, witty, and talkative people. All art is either the wagging of the tongue or of the shameful tail; a writer is an intellectual meddler. The Athenians were the greatest artists in the world; as Thucydides asserts, the men of Athens were born to trouble others.

Greece at the time paid vows to Athene and Artemis, who resembled handsome youths rather than maids. People are less surd to a doctrine or saying of a lewd urchin of Hellas than to one of Plato's, for this is not the age for the piety of George Herbert and the homilies of Izaak Walton, which will have to wait for another century or two to come from their ossuaries. We are ashamed of Anaxagoras, Theophrastus, and the semitic Thales and Eudoxus, and we cover them with darkness where all ignorance and vileness are hid: but in Paradise there is no night. At present, thinkers of antiquity appear to be more dead than the carcass of a mylodon, which is said to contain enough animal matter to give off a flame in a spirit lamp. La Fontaine believed that anyone who preferred his own time to that of the ancients was insane.

Truths and good books have the mold of a freshly dug grave and do not live again until some benign author has the power to say to them, "Come forth, Lazarus!" What booty is there in goodness and learning to the fierce, the expedient, and the world? We relish Homer, among other reasons, because Hera calls Artemis a "shameless bitch," and we would heed Paul's seventh chapter in *Romans* more did we know that he had lain with some hetaera in Greek Tarsus, where he was born. Tarsus is renowned because Cleopatra and Antony had an assignation there. Semiramis snares us more quickly than Paul because man is artistic rather than indignant.

Narcissus despoils the finest intellects of their fruits. No one can love his own image and care for philosophy. Writing is an exceptional vanity, and Solomon put down the fewest words because everything has been said. It is told that Diogenes wrote maybe no more than two dialogues or five at the most. People who hanker after originality are not only not to be trusted but are mad and ignorant. It would be best not to write at all except that people so readily forget what has been said. Worse, they despise oracles that are not brand-new so that a modern author with some skill in employing sentences feigns that he has the latest revelation from Jupiter or Orpheus. Despite long usage hallowed by Thoth and Hermes, some words are harshly scorned like good and evil, justice and virtue, and the only way to present such ideas anew is to show that the sages of Attica were not stale scholiasts or sciolists. It would be cant to describe Diogenes, Crates, and Zeno as saints, though they are sometimes referred to as the fathers of stoicism. They were secular savants for Diogenes asserted that cannibalism was good.

The brain is a poor reed shaken in every wind, and its fruits are the sport of dust. Solomon has said that the making of many books is a great weariness and that there is nothing new under the sun. There are no new books, and had men the least wisdom, they would read what has been written and use the Nile papyrus for shoes and raiment and not for more arrogant writings. It is of much doubt that the trade of letters has done anything else but whet greed and jealousy and hatred. Thoth has died, and the cicadas scorn the present alphabet men because they say they write for themselves although they are as gluttonous to be known as Tantalus in Erebus.

The sick have written astounding books: The poet Schiller was consumptive, and the odor of rotten apples quickened his soul; Hölderlin was insane; and Christopher Smart spent most of his latter days in Bedlam. Donne and Shakespeare, heretical bawds in their heyday, were broken in their fifties. Donne sat in his cerecloth for eight years. These men gave much to other people, and even to the universe, for unless man returns a tithe of what he has taken from nature, he is a skulking grout-head. But no one needs novel miseries, though some cultivate solitude, and most of our books look as though they were ill, lonely, and starved to death. Books should exhale affections, friendship, and good precepts and be redolent of the mulberry, osiers burning in the hearth, or lentils in the pot. The most pernicious volume is a cold one which is not conceived on Mount Ida but comes from the lawless lust of malignant privacies. Crates, seeing a young man walking by himself, said, "Have a care of lewd company." Men unaccustomed to people are savages and are as odorless as the eunuch.

The bad poet is a toady mimicking nature. Many poets and philosophers sat at the table of Dionysius the Tyrant; each one of them inclined his ear somewhat, as though this were the natural way of hearing, because Dionysius was rather deaf.

Dionysius could not refrain from writing tragedies, all of which were horrible. Nor could Plato abstain from visiting Dionysius. Is it credible that Plato expected a sensual carcass like Dionysius to give up his tyranny, which is the desire to rule everybody but one's self?

The good poet, as well as the philosopher, is the guardian and father of the races. Nicander in the *Georgics* is our mentor when he writes: "Terrible evils oftentimes arise from eating olives, or pomegranates, or from the trees of maple or of oak; but the worst of all are the swelling sticky lumps of mushrooms." Nicander also advises us that wild beetroot, sorrel, nettles, spinach, onions, and leeks should be boiled. It is remarkable that Heraclitus, often intemperately obscure and given to such abstractions as the logos, should have left among the smallest fragment of sayings the following: "Oxen are happy when they eat the bitter vetch."

The greatest poets teach many remarkable things, but poems give off a vapor like the tripod which clouds their meanings, and one is just as much gulled by Shakespeare as by a cutpurse, a liar, and an adulterer.

A poet ought not to trust himself, for he is a chameleon, assuming the complexion of his surroundings and has the slavish vices of his time. Pausanias, who displayed awe, which is a great gift, was foolish about the Pentathlon; he showed as much wonder for a statue of Symmachus, a wrestler, or for the inscription on a monument to Cleogenes, who had won a prize with a riding horse from his own stud, as he did for the Dioscuri or primeval Saturn. The maid Artemis grasps a lion in one hand and a leopard in the other, and this may seem to be superstitious and stupid, except to those who realize that only such ferocious beasts prevent men from violating the virgin. We must either judge or go mad; the reverence for the athlete in Pausanias or Pindar is base.

He who is least of all insane is the philosopher. The poet has a more prolific and winelike faculty and is the fountain in which the nurses of Bacchus were said to have washed him when he was born. Socrates was correct when he said that the poet could not explain his verses, for writing is sleep halved by dream—the dream is of a changing, watery substance. The prophetic life of Menelaus is spent on the Nile, grappling with Proteus, who is a river oracle.

Unless the poet goes each day to the Delphic sibyls or studies the oldest customs and laws of men, he is no better than a mime, or a stage singer. Without the aid of philosophy he is a flautist, and he loves only his windpipe.

There are no dogmas, there is only veneration and animal intimation. Pascal said that man is too stupid to invent a worm. He is also too ignorant to admit he is one. It is impossible for man to know anything, and utterly pusillanimous for him to cease striving after knowledge. The sage studies all the days of his vanity to make better mistakes.

The mullet hides his head, imagining he has concealed himself, which is the habit of the mediocre.

The last works of thinkers are sometimes alluded to as their senilia, but this does not mean that these are feeble cries but that they are the fabled songs of death the swan utters in her final throes. The swan is fierce, and no poet hears the hymn of this dying bird without cosmical trembling, and there is as much courage in the swan in its last moments as in Plato's *Laws* written at seventy-five. A story exists that Socrates had a dream of a cygnet and that the next day Plato came to see him. Helen was born from a bird, the offspring of Leda and Zeus, who took the shape of a swan, and she was a great beauty and did as much mischief as divine Plato. As Callimachus held, a great book is a great evil. There is as much malice in genius as good.

No one really invents anything; Homer sings what he has compiled, and he creates neither Ilium, Menelaus, nor Agamemnon but catalogues their deeds in a cadence, for Orpheus and Apollo and Pan are the sweet sounds that come out of pipes, reeds, and flutes; but it is said that Apollo laid aside the lyre to follow Cybele, which means that the earth is more sacred than music. In the ground are the annals of the many leafy races that perish, and Homer, like Apollo, gathers these records which Cybele has in her bosom. Homer had a moral ear rather than merely a pipe or flute.

Plato said that music enslaved the multitude, and people listen to the most consummate sounds either lying on sofas or their faces cast into such rapturous vacancies that it is hard to know whether they have the groaning sleep of a sow or a stygian ecstasy. In this humbug mood of intellectual attention they assume the posture of a disgusting lick-spittle or one of the dwarfs of Domitian. Apollo flayed Marsyas and hung up his skin in a cave because he was a loutish flautist. Piping is a stupid, gossipy art which has spoiled whole countries.

Strabo tells us that the elephants of India could be taught to obey by words and that others were pacified by tunes accompanied with the beating of a drum. Unfortunately, music either puts the mind to sleep or inflames men. Though everyone regards music as a good power, it is often a malefic one, and poets who are more concerned with the ear than with the moral intellect are harmful. Anacreon of Teos was a wine sieve, and much of his poetry was written to praise the tyrant Polycrates.

Most of the *Iliad* is taken up with the war at Troy; many for this reason have thought Homer to be a martial poet, which is untrue. Strife is the god which destroys those who crouch before destiny. Homer readies the soul for fate, and Hesiod prepares it for frugality. Zeus sends penury to man, declared Hesiod, and he who has never laid the osier and the penny fruits and seeds at the altar of indigence has a sluggish ear for the sorrows of the needy.

Man studies philosophy to resist pleasure or reads poetry that he may not grow crabbed or morbid. When Porphyry conversed with his pupils, they often drank wine though he never took any. It is told that Alypius, living about the same time, was almost a pigmy in stature and that he was well-nigh all soul and intelligence, his body being too small for corrupt matter to forage or pasture there. Man at present is far less soul than body; he is hurt in all places, and he walks on his wounds, and this is his pleasure, his pain, and his art. He is not as carnal as he thinks; for though, as Catullus says, he perambulates all beds as though he were the white doves of Zeus, this is the songless, exhausted century. The virgins have gone, chaste Diana has departed, and O Catullus, where are the unblemished youths? Who supplicates Priapus for his powers, or pours out libations to Poseidon? In the *Rig-Veda* man is told not to utter a mundane thought in the morning.

VI

MORE TOWNS AND CITIES are destroyed by sexual disorders than by plagues, famine, and disease. Unless men follow some discipline, they are demented from birth until their demise. Numa Pompilius, seeing how fierce the people had grown because they were always at war, built the fane of Janus, which was open when the cities of Latium were in arms and shut when they were quiet. Numa appointed days for feast and rest, which are called the *fasti*, he divided the year into twelve moons, or months. He paid homage to Jupiter, as the cosmos is sacred, and he did not omit war or chastity, for when men fail to canonize their lusts, they are most brutal. Besides, reverence for the planets and for vestals keeps men still a little while.

Man is not by nature ascetic or domestic; the human anthropoid would be a house dove eating the mast and roosting in the beeches were he not wild. Cyclops is a steadfast eater of men; the rough Solymi are incessantly arrogant; Ares or a javelin is the deity of Magog. It is the irregular outbreaks of passions that are unexpected despots we seldom overwhelm. The fool is wet and parched, beckons one from whom he flees, and is cloyed all in one hour. The hardest man to endure is one's self, and he is the most untrustworthy of foes. If one wears the livery of the meek, he creeps too low, or when one cries out, "My God, I am a gnat," he dilates his throat; the recluse complains because the daughters of Judah do not come to gladden him.

Scylla is a fit of passion which men must try to avoid, as we should endeavor to shun every tumid emotion, wrath, libidinous visions, cupidity, vanity, self-love. Anthisthenes was reported to have said that, if the wise man does anything, he does it in accordance with virtue as a whole.

It is much more difficult to eschew the passions that resemble snow rather than fire. Men with the fewest words break out on a sudden, and without cause, and like Ajax mistake the sheep for Agamemnon, or as Achilles go into combat with the River Scamander. Achilles, whose mother, Thetis, is hoary sea water, has cold wrath.

Man is the most confused beast in the earth; he marvels at the twelve houses of lust Tiberias built at Capri and is unable to abhor Heliogabalus, who kept the snows of Armenia in diverse caves to cool his debauched Roman blankets. Alexander was embalmed in honey, and so are all his acts, because men care more for prodigies than they do for the wise or the just.

Men crave to be plants, shrubs, bog moss because their hearts cry out for quiet; a species of pecten which has no offal would have been Dr. Swift's Elysian morsel. The ordinary man dungs upon his spirit, and there is no niter to cleanse him. Chagrin is the honey and the teacher; never to fail is a ditch and delusion and to go all one's days in the same debauched livery. We endeavor to be abstemious, or never slough a single folly. In Crete there was a plane which never lost its leaves because Zeus lay with Europa under this tree; vice is constant and ripens with age; old mulled sins are the worst; he who has never shed the leaves of his youth is always stupid.

Without genitals or indifferent ones, man is neither rock nor water. Parmenides denied the existence of motion, which is Eros, for whenever men move, they stir up the blood. Augustus required his wife, Livia, to procure women for him because it was too painful for him on occasion not to discharge his inflamed vessels.

Man is more ill-made than are the quadrupeds in many respects. Goaded sorely and torn by his appetites, he envies the goat, who is able to have sexual intercourse all his life. He has the utmost desire to abstain from venery so long as he is capable of enjoying it. Origen deliberately became a *spado* because he knew that, as long as man is tormented by that wallet of shame, he will lie and cozen and scratch himself. Sophocles in his old age had said that he was grateful that that riotous, unruly member no longer bothered him.

Seneca was of the mind that the groans and ejaculations that men fear and tremble for are in themselves trivial and contemptible. Not everyone is Demitris the Cynic, who was said by his adversaries to practice mortification. Epicurus, whose name has come to stand for hedonism, took his sickness as a philosophic discipline, and though he died of the agony of the stone, he expired blessing his fate.

There is no doubt that the sensual is very attractive, and it would be wrong not to set before the reader Lais of Corinth and the Pramnian wine. One cannot hide the pears, the fair Corinthian girls, and hope to inculcate in men a valorous continence by a species of skulking and stealth as if virtue could be taught by robbing men. Everybody has to choose, and one will honor neither a man who abstains from a lust of which he has no knowledge nor a teacher who feigns that pleasure does not exist.

There is much difference between the disgraces of the hot man and the wether, unless the latter has brought this upon himself for virtuous purposes, or nature has made him mild. The neuter has no earth in his faculties or flesh and no innocence; Ovid identified Vesta with the hearth. When Agrippina prepared to poison Claudius, she asked Locusta to make up the decoction but Halotus the eunuch to administer it.

Many of the Sophists were moral teachers who grew more stoical but not after their powers had flagged. What is the good of being Solomon or Aristotle and composing *Ecclesiastes* or the *Metaphysics* if one turns his face to the wall because his penis was not erect in the presence of a chit? If man can make the wisest philosophy and have no satisfaction of it because the pudendum is faithless, then all is lost, and man has no other choice but to be a sparrow or a newt. Nobody recollects pleasure except dimly, for one can remember the shape of a cube or an isoceles triangle but not the color of the nipples of Daphne nor the aches she once gave us.

Asceticism has always attracted the most carnivorous and sexual men. The Socratic head looked like neither the beautiful cranium of Apollo nor that of Buddha. Socrates was a thick-looking man, with the heavy mouth of an orgiast and ugly as Thersites. Want, Poverty and Philosophy are such sages that those who follow these three are often better than men who appear to have the self-abnegating mien. Penury is an accursed blessing, according to Langland's Piers the Plowman.

The young should be nurtured in Sparta, and they should be taught to pray very often, for the navel is no more than the span of a palm from the shameful organ. A rude and hard infancy, according to Balzac, is best for the development of character. Eros is wily, feigning that the whole of human existence can be contained in the table, stool, and bed.

There are many things to be said for the bed provided one does not lie in it all day long; though Zeus could do it with impunity, man cannot. Besides, if a man is not a foolhardy sensualist, he is not likely to weaken the members he so covets that by forty they are a pendulous memorial of quondam pleasures.

"But in every case we must be most upon our guard against what is pleasant, and pleasure," Aristotle writes. Plato said that extreme pleasures and pains produce madness. Delights make men rave. No one knows anything and can only surmise that his knowledge is an ethereal zero. Were it not so, men would be more overweening than they are.

The men that are most interesting are those who have

valiantly resisted the delights for which they ached. Solomon said, "Do not give all your strength to women," which is wise. One does not go to genius to be one of the cripples or the blind at Bethesda, but to be healed and to be seamed together again. The Essenes were craftsmen and healers, and the word means to cure. Luke was also a physician. It is best not to abjure the fruits of the earth if this makes one irascible. A philosopher is a vestal when he rejects what hotly draws him, for the best of men are not those who abstain because they have no testicles but those who attempt to govern that Aetna between their legs. No matter what sage or philosopher or poet we cite, we have to return to the same vexing dilemma: Should man copulate?

It is hard to be Socrates when one has capital testicles, and only a plagiary of virtue if one has not. Who can brag the goodness of a dead phallus? And what bravery is there in the abstemiousness of a man who has a worthless prepuce? Moreover, it is redundant to be temperate when one is already impotent. What is overcome is good, for man has a negative conscience—the monitor or daemon in Socrates' which prevented him from doing wrong, but did not compel him to perform what is right.

Evil, which is our companion all our days, is not to be treated as a foe. It is wrong to cocker vice, but we grow narrow and pithless if we are furtive about it, for this is at best a pretense, and the sage knows good and evil are kindred. The worst of men harm others, and the best injure themselves.

Man is always tempted, and it is what he avoids rather than what he does that enobles his character; the Crees knotted a few willow bushes together, which represented their deity, Kepoochikawn. This is a very rude image of divinity, but less woe and vanity will come of it than from the Zeus of Praxiteles or the temple of Solomon. Cree warriors ate live coals to be gods, and when they suffered pains, drums were beat so that their groans would not be heard.

It is possible to overvalue the ascetic habits, and many will complain that the beast's skin and club of Hercules, Stoic symbol of principles and frugality, are not sufficient for human wit or manners. This is very likely so, and even Seneca, living in the midst of the turpitudes of Nero, said, "I am not yet come to my own frugality." There is much confusion abroad, and our poets are no wiser than the street urchin. This, of course, Plato discerned, and many blame him for setting up a severe fratery, yet there is no man who is not a far greater despot to himself than he believes the laws of Plato's *Republic* to be.

Here is a riddle: If the gospel and many wise books have been written to govern the genitals and to take away the imperial mind from this rugose wallet of mirth, how is it that a boy just growing his pubes and while at chapel, and without the least thought of anything save Mark and Luke, has an erection? This is as much of an enigma as the Ephesian sod, and must be considered along with the lilies and the *Proverbs of Solomon*.

VII

MAN HAS NO positive abiding tenets; his genius is negative, the Socratic *elenchus*, which urges him not to be unjust, intemperate, self-loving, and covetous. "All our errors," said Rochefoucauld, "come from self-flattery." Human skin has no greater wish than to lie among the water lilies and to forget. Lechery enters the understanding heart, for no one can eat of the Tree of Knowledge and be innocent. Images make us cunning and unreliable, but without them we are brutes and stones. The primitive Pelasgians had no knowledge of figures, and they set up unwrought rocks to represent Cronus and Hera, and were natural.

Confucius said that, when people prate much of virtue,

there is none, and when they talk too much of the family, it has decayed, and when they are continually babbling about their homeland, they have already cursed the earth. The most barbaric nations that guarded their countries with shields made out of the skin of the riverhorse cared more for their hearth and wives than does the present anthropoid.

People have almost no will to be simple; the most acute rapture is in being roundabout. The tanner and the potter were in the mind of Socrates when he uttered a precept, and the market place was his fane. Paul's head was thrown into a sheepfold, and the brother of Jesus was killed by the pole of a fuller. The saint's pericranium lies among the lambs; heaven bless the sheep pen and preserve the fuller, lest Paul and James be forgot.

Man is a vast riddle to the gentle heart until he comes to the desolate conclusion that he can do no better than he does. Captain John Smith, who settled the Virginia Plantation, said that his greatest disease was his endeavor to do good. This is a precious malady, and each one should do all he can so to sicken, but he must never forget that he is ailing of virtue.

Yet man remains untamed, and the human being can never gratify his mouth, arms, hands, or feet. His passions are as mixed as the cameleopard or the hippocentaur. The chimera, the unicorn, the harpy, the griffin are different aspects of his chaotic nature. Can one fathom such a creature who is a quadruped, reptile, insect, and bird? He is never of a single brood or tribe. The Achlis who sleeps leaning against a tree arouses envy in him simply because he goes to bed. He will hurry more quickly to starwort or marsh rushes, if he has never eaten them, than to the wild ases relished by Phoebus Apollo. He craves every novelty and is for that reason continually a bane to himself and a surprise to others. Man runs to the lizard, which he is told is an aphrodisiac, although his prostate is already worn out and he is suffering from urinary retention. When informed that in India elephant tusks are used instead of gates, he is rapturous. The ordinary bores him; he reviles the season, the turtle rains, the April leaves which bring him no havoc, nor happiness. God created the day to dispel the void which is the delirium of man.

Nobody is quiet, for tedium is every man's gibbet; ennui makes men pilfer themselves of friends and sack their hopes or the good luck singing in their pockets. Rest in people is unbearable; we are the white malms the frosts and rains crumble into the manure with which we dress our pasture. Man is a bore four seasons of the year, and stupid every day. His character is seldom awake at dawn. Sleep is a coward's mire, and each day is another Circe's sty of inertia.

Almost all trouble comes from impatience. We burn with satiety, which has a use also, for Naples is paved with the lava of Scala. The greatest sorrow is that one believes either there is free will or that there is absolutely none. Not to do anything is an offense against nature, which is always energetic. There is no battle man can wage that is so essential to his intellect as the war against necessity.

Fate turns aside from the lethargic; the Lord of the Psalmist, who breaks the ships of Tarshish with an east wind, is Himself impaired by the sluggard. Man's might is piddling, but the ground hungers for it.

People throw away their heritage and even their lives for no other cause but impatience. We are the meacocks of a grubby destiny because we cannot wait. There are months which are as chaff in the wind, and all our labor is lost. When the long rains settle in the head and the cliffs and headlands within us are covered with fog, we cannot hear Homer.

The ring ouzel winters in mountainous countries; hedgehogs make their hibernacula with leaves and moss, and hempseed contents the swallow. But will apples comfort the heart or the flagons of Cana wine stay ennui? There is no trident to sweep the tides of the soul or univalve in which to catch its surging beat. Virtue often has the ague; the spleen in talent is damaging Danewort.

The affections of human beings are a weather-cock and are turned one way or another by mischance and sickness. Many signs are given to us to indicate that we are rejected; the Latins referred to every door as Janua, and though we know, without thinking, when this door is open or shut, we attempt to pass through it at all times. People give off an intellectual effluvium which draws or chokes us. The vine cannot endure the smell of the cabbage; ivy stifles the oak.

Man falls out with one he loves, discovering that his fresh adversary has canine teeth and that she had smiled too warily to have shown them earlier. After we have ceased to look upon the beloved with hot or inflamed eyes, little that is not gall or dross remains of the quondam inamorata. We remember that her nostrils were puerile and that her mouth was the ejected stomach of a fish when pursuing prey. Only when the affections ebb, do we see the flats and the rubble our tidal emotions had covered; often what looks sloughy and fruitless is our own vacant hearts.

Who can say to his soul, I did not recognize the liar and the thief who took my green herbs and laid waste my furze and haws. Everyone must give himself up to some thought, vision, or *ultima Thule*, or else live torpid and disgrace the ground he treads. It is more important to be a dupe than to be Timon; a man who cannot be deceived is shrewd, which is icy insanity.

Still, the gull enlarges his vices no less than the deceived. He who is not a hunter is the prey. The lurcher ambushes the fallow deer, and each one satisfies the other, because the captive is as ready to be taken as was Theodota the courtesan.

We are not often ready for our friends; some wait for the setting of the Pleiades to give their affections, or say they will act upon knowledge later, which is stomach thinking. The maudlin bask in easy, vernal raptures, which they consider ideas or emotions, but are wind eggs called *zephyria*, birds lay these barren eggs when the soft breezes stroke their feathers. Man hunts the faults of his companions when tedium inflames him, for when nothing happens to man, he looks for disaster, a flood, a hurricane, the death of a loved one; his stupor is gratified by newspapers, the water-closet obsequies of the rout. Men would not require earthquakes, fires, funerals to instruct them were they born wise, for each one has all these tumults within him. But some are of a froward temperament and look to such miserable accidents as fresh experiences. Heraclitus held that war is the father of progress; pain is a deity, a Buddha, or a devil. So long as man is as malformed as he is, he will kill and torment and seek the wheel, the rack, and the scaffold as a remarkable sensation. Affliction is more important to mortals than Ionic luxury, and ill hap is food for the sluggard. The Shulamite of Solomon is the smallest of gratifications to the human biped. Myrrh and unguents and all the spices of Arabia Felix are not enough for him. Mortification and crucifixions draw him greatly. Lucretius asserted that human beings derive unusual felicity from seeing people drown. Each one is relieved because he is not dying, but he also trembles with subtle joy at the sight of the pyre, seeing a man castrated, or witnessing violence.

Many think solitude marvelous though the cemeteries are filled with such contented corpses. Loneliness is the ecstasy of the humbug, for everybody is as alone as he wants to be. The shroud will wrap us up soon enough without hankering after the satisfactions of the shades.

Most men require stern gods if they are not to run mad and be thieves; the stone boundaries were regarded as divinities, and no one dared defile a rock that separated his farm from his neighbor's. These deities or stones which separate one man's property and another's should be well defined in friendship. People should regulate their friendships, for though it melts the heart to sighs and clouds when a companion hastens to our relief, it is better not to expect it. A savant recognizes a foe, a demigod a false friend. A real friend is a doughty warrior, a Hector, who is described by Aeschylus as having a heart softer than a mulberry. There are certain burdens we must keep to ourselves, first of all our lamentations. Few can endure another man's misfortune and sit down with him in his plight and sadly eat together the walnuts of Zeus or rest beneath the beech trees, which Nicander, in the *Georgics*, says are the altars of Pan.

Pindar claims that fortune is one of the Fates; character and misfortune are the same mineral. Each one has title and deed to his miseries. "The ox knoweth his owner, and the ass his master's crib"; the unfortunate sits upon his evil luck until it is hatched.

A Greek Cynic said that one should be prepared to detest

a friend because it was almost certain that he would be a foe. The erudite is no more fervent than the weather-headed fellow. Humble people accept their limitations more quietly and without the vanity of those who are talented. Pedants suppose that the mind is a divinity, but it is less sure than the foot. One knows with some assurance where the foot will go, provided the mind is not guiding it.

People do more to earn a disadvantage than to purchase a benefit. Those who hanker after friends either hawk round them as though they were their prey or, disappointed, mew themselves up in a room called society. A disorderly biped, man is as sloven in his discontent as he is in his pleasant, leafy summers. The blackthorn blossoms when a cold north-eastern wind rears its branches; the sand martins lie torpid and without food amidst their *latebrae* until the sun beckons them again.

Fragrant skin fetches the hypocrite and the fleshmonger. We invite flesh, pleasant underwear, costly socks to our homes; the guest in the house of the Pharisee spreads the odor of myrrh, cassia, and Arabian balsam, though aromatic plants flee from hard weather. The wild olive at Olympia is one of the most perdurable trees, but this is the fruit of Pallas Athene who is wisdom. Does one ever find out who is a pond, desert, or ocean shrub? Moonflower, goat willow, duckweed are lake plants; botany gives us assurances which men do not. Can one guess who is loyal? Suffering Job is eaten up by his friends.

Men are more jealous than birds or quadrupeds because they are the prisoners of revenge and envy. Even the Greek soothsayers were covetous. Calchas died of vexation because Mopsus was a better prophet than he was.

Man is most easily wounded because he mistakes an asp or

fox for a friend. It is simpler for Hercules to carry out the dung from the Augean stables than to cast out the bile of an antagonist. Livia detested Germanicus for no other reason except that her joints were old and rancid and filled with spleen whilst he was modest and young. This hapless prince had earned the vilest thoughts from his brother, whom he had aided and never harmed.

Germanicus had a gentle disposition, but his brother was rapacious Tiberius, and his grandmother, the malevolent Livia. Tiberias practiced every cunning, so that his liberal acts made him an impostor among the Romans. The Parthians despised him for having a sluggish interest in horses, in the chase, and because the humblest subject could see him without much hindrance.

Piso was another viper among the hedges who awaited the death of Germanicus. Nature was tardy in satisfying Piso. What he could not accomplish by poison he expected to gain by spells and the effect of baleful portents upon the fevered mind and body of Germanicus. Piso commanded his lictors to bring exhumed corpses upon which were inscribed the name of Germanicus into the room where the prince was confined; should his vitality not be squandered by the disease, then theses evil omens would attack his reason and madness would force him to quit this life.

The lion and the eagle and the crocodile are not the peers of Tiberius, Livia, or Piso. The male crocodiles kill each other to possess the female, who shows a considerable attachment for her young. The lion is malicious when his teeth are anile, because he is no longer vigorous enough to attack any one as effectively as man.

Tired men are the most perfidious; the weak are foul enemies and dissemblers whose canorous words about the good and the true are the covert for their corruption. Always infants in vileness and abominations which never grow any taller, for yea, they are the sucklings out of whose mouths come the innocent filths.

Man seldom relinquishes a single fault he condemns in others; for he is deaf to a rebuke. He covets what he does not want; alas, the bread he casts upon the water is returned to him. Most of the time is given to improving his vices; he cannot bear to be taken for a simpleton in the game of malice. When the viper is unable to poison his victim, he fetches his whole brood to pour out their venom with more success. When the fangs are not shown at once, we do not know where they are; the teeth of the polypus are between her feet.

It is told that, when a viper eats a scorpion, its bite is fatal; whether true or not, this is enough to cause the guileless to hide and the wicked to kill. There is no remedy for deceit or venom. Aristotle tells of the plant silphium, in which nests a serpent whose spittle destroys life unless one takes a small stone out of the tomb of an ancient king and pounds and mixes it in wine and drinks it. The stone is supposed to be asafetida, but this is a fable, for there is no decoction in the tomb or anywhere else to cure one of the serpent's bile.

Men of earth and water are sundered and perplexed. Fish and man are Dagon, the obelisk is Baal. The Tree of Knowledge is the accursed Serpent, and he who eats of it will creep in the dust forever; his head shall not be honest with his foot, and his hands shall be both the cherub and the raven; his tongue shall be confusion, fox, and shame; he shall be as Balaam, who flogged the ass that saw the angel. Mischance and the vulture are constant, but pleasant tidings drink up the pity in mortals.

VIII

THE AMERICAN IS a treeless ghost. Without ocean or ground, he raves for sea salt and cries out for the palms. The forests howl in the human brute; his arms and feet languish for want of clay and gravel; what can quiet this houseless spirit?

Man is the loneliest worm, and there is no spider or reptile so desolate as Aristotle's forlorn featherless biped. Porpoises sport in pairs, dolphins swim together in the Amazon and in the shoaly water at the mouth of the Tocantins. The *Midas argentatus* frolic with one another along the cacao branches.

But no beast is as placeless as the human being; the ouakari monkeys are found only on the banks of the Japura; taken from their native woods, they grow peevish and die of a lung disorder. The Juris and Passés perish of consumption after the least contact with the treeless white man.

One's origins matter most. Strangers are crazy to be indigenous; what soil or clime is their aliment they do not know. The mud of wells produces the ascarides; palms dote on salt, and fishermen anoint the holes of rocks to catch the Testacea which live in them. The Gospel of Matthew is impregnated with the salt of coastal Judea. Christ is the fish, Pisces, the salt-water star. Mud, fuci, saline quagmire satisfy some minds. Once men forsake their sources, a race of deceivers is spawned.

Men are beggars in desolation. Overwhelmed by sorrow or need, they reveal their beginnings. Do we learn what element prevails within us, whether we are a range of hills, and when we are at flood tide? Denials are our half-wild cattle in the mighty Amazon which drown, starve, or are the booty of the alligators. No one can go beyond the confines of himself.

A river has an entire identity which a Ptolemy or a Juba can know, and at its source it is mild and can be forded; man is marl, a sandy campo, and he is broken into many fragments by his sundry inceptions. Indians on the banks of the Japura fall ill when the Solimões breathes the detritus of their clay and vegetable mold upon them.

The white man is a captive of the new continent, according to William Carlos Williams, the only poet with the historian's faculty of the American earth. The beginnings of the American are a Babel to himself. A stranger in the earth, he exudes the sullen weather of New York, which has no dry heat or austere winter. The North American Caliban, neither hot nor cold, cannot attach himself to his neighbor;

and solitude is fatal to the affections. The Canadian Indians, after losing their kindred, tore up their tents, destroyed their possessions, and wailed together.

The treeless paleface cannot come to the ground; the mountains do not know him, and the mesa has forgotten him. Few and meager are the legends in the new land. The naturalist has called a tree of Brazil the *Cecropia*, which is the food of the sloth. This serpent tree, for the ancient Cecrops was a human snake, nourishes the sloven.

The *Pelopaeus* wasp has working songs, one when he carries the clay in his mandibles and another after this labor is done. What chant is there for drudgery in North America? Who molts his infamy or flowers: June and July leaf the campos; can tedium produce seeds for herons and storks?

The vampire bat devours the acajous and guavas, but the table of North America is sick. The songless hands of its natives are rude in amours; they have no time to savor the bride and to faint with love for her flesh and her delicate garments. The wings of the greenfinch are wounded when hungry for mating, and the cock snipe and windhover languish.

Impotency is growing apace in the New World, and the womb is barren. Without progeny the male is a grub; childless wedlock is the earthen jar which can never be filled with the Cana wine. Turtles, unable to hatch their eggs, scatter them in despair over the swamps.

Indian women strew their clothes with the feathers of the uirapara as a philtre. Anoint the fingers with mandragora; Leah's teats are starveling fruits, and her belly as seedless as the orchard graft, the stoneless grape, and the hybrid orange. God return the natural vintage and the citrous branch of Mesopotamia and Brazil.

We waver between equatorial weather and the poles; the moral man is as amphibious as the asphodel or the squill, land and sea plants. The irresolute long to winter on a Canadian bog covered with willows, larch, and spruce. The rich muse upon paintings of Eskimo sails made of whale gut, but this is the sleep whose seeds are scattered in dry ravines.

People in the new continent have no constant temperature or nature because they are placeless; transplanted persons suffer most from the disease of moroseness. The Indian, a cleft Tartar, sickens easily in moist Brazil.

Boys in America, often gentle before coming into their *virilia*, grow fierce and sullen within two to three years. Indians with a tractable disposition disappear after puberty, spending the rest of their lives in the *sertão* or by the banks of feral rivers. Trees depend upon the sites rather than their fruits or seeds to sire good progeny. The ash or poplar, and the olive on Parnassus, are the hardiest; mountain or forest wood is least corrupt. The seeds of sweet pomegranate produce a depraved tree. The sorb is sterile if removed to a warm vale; it is alleged that water snakes change into vipers when the marshes are parched.

Wild people ripen late and seldom bear fruit. The North American is a cold, hilly race; in his beginnings he had a snowy vigor; Thoreau, Whitman, and Melville are Olympian trees, half-cultivated but doughty. The cypress grows on Mount Ida, the terebinth springs up on rough Syrian slopes; silver fir, the valonia oak, and the kermes oak seek their home on the flanks of ranges.

Oak and plane have deep roots; the trees of pleasure, olive and pomegranate, shallow ones. Papyrus makes men vainglorious, and it grows in the shoals. Hardihood and loyal traits repel the comfortable; mountain trees are sturdy and rough; lakes are congenial, indolent friends, but they do not enliven us. People use each other, which nature and love allow. The toady drains his benefactor, the lover dilates his force. Human beings and nations are no different from insects and trees.

The Quiché Maya Codex is jaguar psalms. Aztec hieroglyphs are water demons and the human skulls sacrificed in the oratories. Thoreau's precepts are the strongest books of the American smell of the slime, the horny spicules of sponges, and the spermaceti of leviathan.

IX

MEN TRAVEL in search of strange hemispheres, little suspecting that they are ransacking their origins. Doom was the loot of the conquerer; he gathered ruin, misfortune, and death. We are so astonished by men gorged with the calamities of the world that knowledge of their rueful pilgrimage gives us pleasure rather than sorrow.

Juan Ponce de León came to the American coast on Easter and, with what thoughts he had of the lilies of Christ or of Prosperine can only be guessed, called the land *Florida*, or the coming up of flowers. In 1521 Ponce de León returned to Florida, and landing, he received a mortal wound in the thigh and died a few days later in Cuba.

Francisco de Córdoba arrived with one hundred Spaniards, and in sore need of water went ashore; one drank until he was bloated and died; other soldiers were killed by Indians; Córdoba died from wounds shortly after his return to Hispaniola.

In 1521 Lucas Vásquez de Ayllón set out in two vessels for the mainland, looking for the man-eating Caribs to work in the mines of the Antilles. He saw cultivated pearls, which shook his reason. No one can see what the albatross eats, and avaricious Christians have no less skill than this carrion feeder. Reaching the province of Chicora, he went inland, where he saw very white Indian giants. By a ruse he got one hundred and thirty Indians to board his ships and then set sail for Hispaniola. But almost all the natives perished, sorrowing for their wives and children and maize fields.

Lucas Vásquez set out a second time for the continent of Florida, and took his pilot Miruelo. Unable to find Chicora, the pilot succumbed to the watery fever known as melancholy, and died insane.

Vásquez again came to Florida in 1524. He despatched two hundred of his Spaniards to a village not more than a league from the Florida coast, and the Indians received the Spanish soldiers with great affection, feasting them for four days; and when their guests were glutted with maize, fish, and meat, they killed them.

Pánfilo de Narváez, the *adelantado* of Florida, left San Lucar with five vessels, and six hundred men to pacify Florida to the Rio de los Palmas. When he arrived at Hispaniola, only one hundred and eighty men were alive. After procuring more men and supplies in Cuba, he sailed to the Bay of Santa Cruz with three hundred men and forty-two horses; shortly after one vessel was lost on the fierce coast.

From the beginning, Narváez's men were scathed by the sea and the tempests, which blew continually into their heads and bowels. After one storm they found the small boat of a ship in the branches of a tree and sixty dead Spaniards with faces raveled and distorted from beating against the rocks. The trees were riven and prone, the earth sour and sere, and the grass and the leaf were slain by sea salt and the black angelic winds.

Pánfilo Narváez had been told by the Indians there were gold and silver in Apalaché; the three hundred Spaniards led by Narváez walked in bitter sea water to Apalaché, which was in northwestern Florida and extends from Pensacola to the Ocilla River. With nothing to eat but two pounds of biscuit and a half a pound of bacon, as an allowance for fifteen days, they were as dejected as the forty-two horses that had survived the Florida gales. But they were still callow in the pangs of woe.

They came to the Suwannee River, whose violent and sinister current took hold of a Spaniard and his horse, drowning both of them. The men grieved over their companion, but the horse they ate for supper that night.

At Apalaché there was dry maize, and forty low huts of thatch surrounded by forests, lagoons, and fenny ground. Cedar, evergreen oak, savin, the palmetto, and the alligator tree were abundant. There were deer, hares, lions, and a small brute with a pouch on its belly, besides night herons, partridges, merlins, sparrow hawks, mallards, and gerfalcons. The Indians went naked, were well-made of body, and had arrows, thick as the arm, which they shot with precision. There were forest, quagmire, and mountain cat, with beans and pumpkins in the fields, but no Patagonian ore. In place of gold and silver they saw raw, wooden mortars in which maize was cracked; it was a nine days journey on foot through lagoon water reaching up to the paps to come to the pumpkins, maize, and beans of Auté.

Pánfilo Narváez was in so doleful a condition, his hopes weaker than his legs, that he asked his men how they could retire from earth so malign. The Spaniards repaired to a water of sorrows they called the Bay of Horses. Here they wept and slew the poor brutes they had to eat. Without tools, iron, or forge, they made pipes out of wood which with deer skins they shaped into bellows; stirrups, spurs, and crossbows were cut and beaten into nails, saws, and axes. They had resolved to quit the land in five barges, which had to be built. The boats were calked with the fiber of the dwarf palm; rope and rigging came from horses' tails and manes. The savins provided the oars. There was scarce any rock for ballast or anchor, and no mountains to strengthen their will. The country was morass, without hills or summits foaled by Ocean. A sterile lava peak gems the mind, for in Scoriae amber grows.

They flayed the legs of the horses, using the skins for water bottles. They foraged for shellfish in coves and creeks, but forty died of hunger; others were ambushed by the naked giant archers in the reeds.

There is the Maya goddess of suicide, Ixcab, who is the patroness of men hindered by evil stars. The Spaniards, kindled by ruin, had no such deity, and none did harm to themselves. Some found shellfish, and the Indians killed ten who were digging in ravines or in creeks for food. In the haven at the Bay of Horses there were dried mullet and roses, which relieved them. The bottles made out of the horses' legs rotted, and they were without water for five days. A few swallowed sea salt, and three or four died crazy. The storm never stopped, blowing and beating them into twisted, gaunt skin. At Pensacola Bay a canoe of Indians was sighted. When they visited these natives, they found clay jars of water and a pile of dried fish set outside the savage hovels. The cacique gave them fish and water, and the Spaniards brought them the maize they had, and they ate in one another's presence. At midnight the Indians fell upon the sleeping Spaniards, massacring as many as they could.

Setting sail in their barges, they entered an estuary and saw other Indians in a canoe, who wore their hair long and loose and were robed in martens, heavy with musk.

Cabeza de Vaca, in the first boat, came upon the great waters of the Mississippi, which De Soto saw fourteen years later. To the Spaniards it was *Espiritu Sancto*, or the River of the Holy Ghost; the priest Marquette called it *Concepción*. The great river was as holy to La Salle and Joutel as the map of the earth was to Ptolemy. Cabeza de Vaca was treasurer and high sheriff of the Narváez expedition and a grandson of the conqueror of the Grand Canary. His fable is wilder and more epic than the twenty years of sorrow of Odysseus.

The north wind drove them out to sea, where they ranged the wild ocean for three days, living on half a handful of maize a day. At the Mississippi Delta Pánfilo Narváez and two others, in a boat without food or water and no anchor except a stone, were blown out to sea and never heard of again. By sunset of the fourth day the others with Cabeza de Vaca were near death and lay crumpled upon one another in the barge. At evening they sighted the shore, and crawled from the boat on their hands and knees. There was rainwater in a ravine, where they made a fire, parching some of the maize. Then the boat sank, drowning three of them. The

Indians, viewing the groveling heap of dying men, were so smitten with sorrow for them that they sat on the ground and howled for their misery like animals in the wilderness.

The Spaniards named the island Malhado, meaning misfortune. The Castilians called coves, straits, and great brute waters by the softest names to woo the Virgin Mary or Saint James or the elements. On the border between Guatemala and Honduras one of the cruelest rapids is Gracias a Dios.

Worse than the forests and the seas was hunger. When their companions perished, the living dried and preserved the cadavers, and cut them into collops for food. The Indians on the island, who gathered up the dust of their dead and drank it with water as a funeral rite, regarded the Spaniards who ate each other with horror.

The natives of Malhado were nude, the women alone covering some parts of their person with wool they plucked from a tree. When they visited one another they remained silent half on hour, and frequently wept when they crossed the threshold of a friend. They cured the sick by blowing and breathing upon them, and demanded that the Spaniards, more dead than alive, drive out the infirmities of those that were ill. When Cabeza de Vaca and his companions said they had no experience in such arts, they refused to give them any food. The Spaniards were in a sore perplexity; either they had to touch the blind, the infected, and the hurt, or they must perish.

Of the many sorrows of men none is more piercing than the cry of the red savages on the Island of Doom. "Touch me that I may be healed!" Not Solomon's chant of fatigue, nor Job's desolation on the muckheap is so great a burden for man to bear as isolation. Concord lies on a swamp, and the Puritans, building it in the wilderness, suffered more from the strokes of loneliness than they did from the bog and the briars. The pilgrims at Plymouth Plantation were stricken by spasms of desolation though they were together.

Solitude is the frontier's sign of Cain; Cain was sent into the woods of Nod for his fratricidal sin. The nomadic habit had become so dominant among the red peoples that children often deserted their parents to wander in thickets, having no other food but palm cabbage, berries, and roots. The Greeks and Romans looked upon barbarians as banished men who had been driven into the forests. Here was the stigma of the dispersion. Hordes, deriving from countless nations, from Abraham and Magog, or Scythia, from Cush or Ethiopia, from Ham or Africa, and from Mizraim or Egypt, were to make their epitaphs in America. These were the ruins of Asia, and the small wreck of Europeans who had fallen into a spurious infancy. These people living savage, aged slowly; the wrinkles of Tiresias or of Nestor came late to the Indian because his faculty is sluggish from long disuse.

After the men left the Isle of Doom, they went naked and cast their skins twice a year like serpents. Cabeza de Vaca peddled pine cones, stones, the sea snail, and conch in exchange for deerskin, maize, beans, canes, and the ocher with which the Indians rubbed their faces. Sometime in April de Vaca and his companions went down the coast, going barefoot among the marshes and the creeks which flow into the Gulf, subsisting on crabs and rockweed. They were in the land of indigence.

On their way toward the Colorado River, they encountered Indians, mostly blind, like the Bosphorus Cimmerians in the *Odyssey*. The neighbors of these eyeless savages were the Yguazes, who threw their female children to dogs so that their enemies could not marry them and become powerful. When an Yguazes had a bad dream, he destroyed his male child. These people bought a common wife for a bow, but a very good one for two arrows. They held marriage of little account, and had connection with women whenever they desired. These natives lived on roots, which gave them fierce pangs in their intestines, and they ate lizards, salamanders, ants, earth, wood, and deer dung. The women spent the nights baking roots in the ovens, while the men drank a liquor made from the mescal button, which brought about ecstatic torpor. Despite the stepmother ground, which starved them most of the year, and contrary to all laws of nature, the Yguazes were a jocular people and rioted during the prickly-pear season. They were a Texas tribe as ferocious as the Teyas, after whom that state takes its name. These savages had slain three of the Christians for going from one hovel to another. By now the Narváez expedition had dwindled to four men, Cabeza de Vaca, Castillo Maldonado, Andrés Dorantes, and Estevanico the blackamoor.

The wandering healers had a retinue of three to four thousand Indians. Out of the Indians' larder of dearth they provided spiders and worms, having nothing for their own children who were suckled until they were twelve because there was hardly any other nourishment for them. Hunger and want made the Indian and the horse restless and nomadic; the North American Indian tied a board around his abdomen when he had no food; hunger is a god of few legends. Poverty, when shared, is a wound that can be cured by a calabash of water or a tea brewed of oak leaves.

The palsied and the cold wanted to put their hands on

de Vaca's arm, breast, or foot. In the eight years of wandering he seldom wore a garment, and when he returned to Mexico City and the Viceroy gave him clothes, he could not endure them nor sleep anywhere except on the ground.

These savages begged Cabeza de Vaca to dissolve a stupor, a pain in the head or entrails; one was said to be dead, for the natives threw down his hut—which meant the sun no longer knew him—but when Cabeza de Vaca touched him, he arose and walked. The sick announced that they were sound when he blew upon their hurts. Among the Maya of Yucatán the ashes of a red parrot's feathers were regarded as a cure for yellow fever. But what nostrum is there for the castaways in the earth save the loving hand? Is there a medicine for the outcast, more dead than stones, who know not when the fish spawn nor how to garner the resin out of the trees? What can be done for these strangers who wean themselves from sunrise?

The western people have sepulchered away the sun and the moon; and the American is far from the Indian rivers, bays, rain, and maize that give him images, without which he is sourceless. Until he is connected with the fens, the ravines, the stars, he is more solitary than any beast. Man is a god, and kin to men, when he is a river, a mountain, a horse, a moon.

For seventeen days, in the plains between the ranges of the Sierra Madre, de Vaca and his companions' fare was a handful of deer suet each day. Then they found the Opata tribes of Sonora, who ate nothing for a third part of the year but powdered rush and straw. At one settlement, on the Rio Sonora, the three white healers, and the Berber, Estevanico, received six hundred hearts of deer in gratitude for touching the natives!

Cabeza de Vaca's pilgrimage is a wild fable of nakedness and love; it is the primitive American scripture of pioneer men in exile together. When Cristóbal Colón arrived, there was no livestock in the new hemisphere. On his second voyage he carried with him five brood mares and twenty stallions. De Soto brought thirteen pigs to Florida. Coronado, marching through Kansas, found the wild progeny of De Soto's sows. It is told that Pedro Mendoza turned five mares and seven horses loose in Buenos Aires some time after 1535 and that their issue ran mad in great droves over the pampas; by 1600 the Patagonians were horsemen. Cabeza de Vaca and Coronado after him had seen the bison, which they called the woolly cow. Mnevis and Serapis were the sacred bulls of Osiris; when Poseidon lay with Ceres, she conceived a horse. Hindu writing is meditative, and the domestic heifer is sacred and near the Buddha. The American legend is the mesa and the bison; it is the myth of a tragic terrain stalked by banished men.

X

EARTH, said to be somewhere in the Sea of Darkness, was known as Antilia, or Antilles, the name later given to the West Indies. De Soto, sacking Golconda, had been unable to persuade Cabeza de Vaca to join him. The Opatas of Sonora had told Estevanico of the seven emerald pueblos in New Mexico. Sesame is yellow, which is one of the colors in Paradise. The carbuncle burns in Eden, and the emerald is as green as the leek. Pliny thought Elysium was an empurpled island.

Antonio de Mendoza, Viceroy of Mexico, dispatched Fray Marcos and Estevanico to Cíbola. The friar, old and in poor health, sent the blackamoor, eager for fame, ahead while he dawdled, ate, and gathered more Cíbola apocrypha.

Indian couriers arrived every few days with astounding tidings from Estevanico which nourished the sleepy ears of the monk. The friar had never been tutored by the Gospels of Quetzalcoatl, the god who taught the Aztecs to pierce the sinning tongue. Estevanico, accoutered with rattles, feathers, and turquoise, carrying a shaman's gourd and surrounded by a large covey of concubines, arrived in Cíbola. He was killed almost immediately. Some say that the Zuñis were hostile to the alien gourd supposed to have curative properties, others relate that Estevanico's retinue of paramours aroused ill feeling. The reason for his death is as obscure as the Fray Marcos *Relación*, which Cortés said was spurious.

The sick monk claimed to have made the pilgrimage from Compostela to the New Mexico settlements on foot in far less time than it took the mounted Spanish in Coronado's expedition. Coronado took a large herd of sheep, whose hooves were worn to the quick after one-third of the journey over the foothills and mesa to Cíbola. The Fray Marcos *Relación* is *tabula rasa* geography, without even the specters of rivers and mountain ranges or the odor and stigma of the *despoblado*, the starved, untilled plains and forest tracts the monk mentions.

Baltasar de Gallegos, the castellan of de Soto, had sold his houses, vineyards, a rent of wheat, and the olive fields in Seville, to seek Jason's fortune. Cortés had made a journey to lower California, in quest of Cíbola. When the friar returned to Mexico City, giving such bloated reports of the vast riches of the southwest Indians, the Viceroy selected a gentleman from Salamanca, Francisco Vásquez de Coronado, to lead an army to that realm.

In 1540 Coronado started his march at Compostela, accompanied by three hundred Spaniards, eight hundred natives, a pair of friars, including Marcos, and plump horses. The army, passing through morose and pelting towns, Chiametla, Culiacán, was particularly dispirited when reaching Chichilticalli, noised to be a famous city but which consisted of a roofless house built of red earth. The Red House, which is what it means in Aztec, marked the beginning of the wild, peopleless regions.

The men went farther into the rough Sierras, where they saw mountain goats galloping in flocks of more than one hundred each. Instead of the palm wine of Babylon, the Spaniards drank the milk of the serpent cactus fruit, which gave them violent fevers. After fifteen days in the forests, the Spaniards reached the Zuñi River, and shortly after that they came to a drab village, containing a small assortment of houses three or four stories high, which was Cíbola. The soldiers wanted to kill the monk Marcos, who was hurried back to Mexico City by Coronado. The pueblo, now in ruins, was Hawikuh, the first of the seven legendary cities. Cíbola, like Quetzalcoatl, the issue of dust and rain, was no god or Chichen Itza.

After a skirmish with the Indians, Coronado took possession of the little adobe town of terraced houses with no streets. Coronado then sent out a party to find his ships lost in the Gulf of California. They came upon nude giants who appeared to be as tall as the Patagonians whom Magellan had encountered. These giants lived in underground huts of straw, baked their loaves in ashes, and were men of immense strength, loading on their heads a fardel of three to four hundred pounds. They went naked despite the great cold, and carried a firebrand to keep themselves warm. The Spaniards, desiring to build barges of reed, asked the giants to help them, and they were most obliging, as they hoped to catch the soldiers on the water and drown them. After a battle with these human towers of Sonora, the men returned to the army.

Coronado remained at Cíbola, while one group of about twenty soldiers went to the Grand Canyon. It is parched land of twisted scrub pines, and well-nigh waterless. The Indian women carried gourds of water, which were buried in the ground along the route so that on the return none would sicken of thirst.

Other Spaniards found the village Acoma atop a rocky mesa. The Indians rubbed the sweat of the horses on themselves to show that they desired peace. When one of these earthen men wished to express his sorrow for a misdeed, he wept, meaning that he intended to be docile. The natives at Acoma brought the Spaniards maize loaves, piñon nuts, cornmeal, and tanned deerskins, and led them into the town playing drums and flutes.

It snowed ten days, covering the junipers and pines. When the army encamped, the horses stood half-buried in it. The snow was so dry that it lay over the soldiers sleeping on the ground as a warm blanket. A dead turkey cock will not molder or give off a bad smell for sixty days because the air is so dry in this country, and the same is true of a dead man. The sky of Quito, the ancient Inca city, has a similar piercing purity that makes men walk the earth as though they contained the cosmos.

The Spaniards arrived next at Tiguex. The pueblos in

this region have no streets, and as the houses are without doors, the only access to the village was up a ladder to the roof. The natives, like the pre-Christian Essenes, excreted at a distance from the settlement. Thy had kivas, which are underground religious chambers, and a corn room containing a trough with three stones: one the women broke the corn with, the other was to grind it, and the third to grind it again.

Tiguex, as well as the pueblos of Cíbola, had an estufa, which is a hot talk room where men gathered together for counsel. There is a great deal of sense to this, as cold conversation brings men tombs, mischief, and wars, instead of friendship. The women cover themselves entirely, and are shown the most tender regard. When a man wishes to marry, he weaves a blanket, placing it before the woman he desires to be his bride, and like Ruth sleeping at the foot of Boaz on the granary floor, she covers herself with it and becomes his wife.

A Spaniard at Tiguex, observing a pretty Indian woman, asked her husband to hold his horse while he pretended to go to the village but instead ravished the wife. The Indians took their vengeance by driving the horses toward the pueblo, shooting arrows at them, and killing many, including seven of Coronado's mules. The Indian nations of the Americas looked upon the horse as a divine brute. After Cortés had left a lame horse in Guatemala, the Maya brought him fowl, meat, and flowers, which killed the animal.

After the Indian woman was violated, a fifty-day battle followed. The natives then surrendered because their water failed. There is so little rainfall in this country that the inhabitants at Tiguex made the mortar for the adobe bricks with human urine. The Iberians, forefathers of the Spanish, scrubbed their teeth with urine according to Catullus and Diodorus.

The Indians had no guileful marriage practices. The converted Aztecs came to the church to be married followed by so many mistresses that the priests sometimes joined the wrong man and woman to each other. When the Aztec was asked to give up his concubines, he said the Spaniards had many women too. The monks replied that these were the servants of the Christians, to which the Indians answered, "The women we keep are our servants also."

The nomadic, coastal Indians cohabited with women at random. The damsels of one tribe were regarded as communal prostitutes until they were wives. In the province of Culiacán, where Coronado's soldiers were for several days, the women who wished to remain unmarried were given subtle clothes and turquoise and placed in a house, and anybody who wanted to go in and lie with one of them could, so that she was not wasted. Men bought their wives on market days. After she was purchased, the chief cohabited with her first, and if he could not deflower her, the price was returned to the man.

At Petatlán, in the province of Culiacán, the women dressed in petticoats of tanned deerskin; in one of the islands in the South Seas the women wore a shift made of the rind of a tree; at Massana, which Magellan visited, the girls were very pretty, adorned only with a small girdle of palm-tree cloth. In Cicuye, the largest pueblo in New Mexico, the virgins, despite the severe weather, went naked until they took husbands. The Aztecs were lascivious but buried their spouses with the spindle and distaff, indicating their respect for feminine virtue. The Quiché Maya held that the flesh of woman was first made of rushes, which can be woven into a basket for fruit or a maiden.

After the siege of Tiguex had ended, one band of soldiers went to look for the Gulf of Mexico. The army under Coronado was ordered to start for Quivira, another legendary Patagonia. On the route they came to a settlement of Querechos, the old name of the eastern Apaches, who lived in tents of bison skins. The Querechos did not sow maize, or eat bread, but lived on raw meat and fruit; they opened the belly of the bison, squeezed out the sodden grass, and drank the juice that was left. They carried the gut of a buffalo filled with blood around their necks to slake their thirst when traveling through the deserts. The Querechos waited till the sun rose and then shot an arrow in the direction they desired to go.

Coronado's soldiers had to drop the bones and dung of the bison on the prairie to make a trail for lost game hunters. Right after prairie grass is trampled upon it waxes stiff. One thousand horses, five hundred bison, five thousand rams and ewes, Coronado's army, and fifteen hundred Indians passed over the mesa grass without leaving a record of one foot or a hoof.

The men reached Quivira, which lay in Nebraska and Kansas. Instead of the one-and-a-half-foot ruby of the great Khan of Cathay, they found plums, grapes, nuts, and flax. The journey was a wretched failure, and Coronado was in disgrace with the Viceroy at Mexico City. The soldiers had known invincible sufferings, and going back to Culiacán and Compostela, half-naked and lice-ridden, they had the satisfaction of the hopeless solely gratified by the prodigies of the New World. Numerous men had been sorely wounded by the poisoned arrows of a fierce, hilly tribe, and all died when struck until they were told by a native to drink the juice of wild quince.

XI

DE SOTO HAD ACHIEVED an odyssey though his deeds were ferine; his darkest acts were healed by the strength with which he committed them. He found the Mississippi River, but he lost an India in pearls because he was amorous.

The vessels in de Soto's armada bore the names of saints, and the appellations of the inlets and coves are the homage they paid to their misfortunes. The Bay of the Holy Spirit and the River of Discords are the sighs of these geographers. They wanted to own *Tierra Nueva*, and for their evil desires the place was translated into a nemesis instead of an angel, and most of them perished or were deprived of their wits.

The discoverers came to rob the ground and streams of

their minerals. Locality was a god to the Indian caciques, who had the names of the rivers, the hills, or the forests where they abode. There was hostility between one Indian settlement and another, and the victors decapitated their enemies, enslaved their wives and children, but seldom took the land.

De Soto, a most civil Iago, gave the Indian *curaca*, or lord, silks, mirrors, and shirts, and embraced him with the greatest affection. He commanded his cavalry to ride as a martial battalion, and the natives thought the horse and man were a single beast. The *curaca* bowed low, kissing the hands of the *adelantado* de Soto, and his Indians came with maize, grapes, dried prunes, fish, and marten furs, while the warriors hid in the forests or near lagoons, their bows and arrows covered by grass.

The Floridians were tall, more than two yards in length, and the Inca Garcilaso de la Vega related that the giant Tascaluza had a waistline that was more than two-thirds of a metre. The men had handsome, brutal countenances, and wore just enough chamois cloth to conceal their haunches and secret parts. The women covered their whole bodies with chamois. Their bows, made of oak, were as hard to draw as the one which Odysseus alone had the strength to use against the suitors of Penelope.

The littoral regions were marshland, and the tumid rivers rose as high as sixty leagues. The maritime soil was so barren that there were times when the Spaniards lived on sea snails and booby birds. The Spanish soldiers in Yucatán and Guatemala ate the inside of the *kunché* bark, which is mellow and soft.

Acorn was his forest milk, of chestnuts he kneaded wild bread, athirst he died mad in the salt estuaries, and hungry, no frigate bird pecked more damage; his burial site was the trunk of a tree or a swamp. Mountain roots, amaranth, unsown rye purge the eye, hyssop and gall and ravine strengthen the knees: He was a Hercules whose works were evil.

Before Hernando de Soto had proclaimed the Kingdom of Florida a possession of Emperor Charles the Fifth, the Cacique Hirrihigua seized four Spaniards who had come to this province with Pánfilo de Narváez. He took them to the plaza of the village, commanding them to run while the Indians shot arrows at them. This gave him such pleasure that he ordered his warriors to torture Juan Ortiz, an eighteen-year-old "fledgling cavalier," but his wife and three daughters beseeched the cacique to spare him, and because of their tender entreaties, he interrupted this spectacle.

Hirrihigua had received some injustices from the Spaniards, who had thrown his mother to the dogs to be eaten; when the cacique had occasion to blow his nose, he could not find it. De Soto had cut off the lips and chins of Indians and severed the heads of fainting couriers rather than trouble to untie the iron collars to which they were yoked. De Soto's Spaniards had seized an Indian guide to lead them back to the bay. After marching in a circle through woods and bogs, eating roots and grass for many days, and discovering that they had been deceived, they threatened to give the Indian to the mastiffs if he did not take them back to the sea, which was only several leagues away. He promised to obey them, and circling the forests again and making the Spaniards endure more terrible suffering, he was thrown to the dogs, who devoured him.

Hernando de Soto took the greatest pains to gain kind deeds of the cacique Vitachuco, who had sent many messengers to him, promising that he would command the ground and hills to swallow the Spaniards; he had also ordered the birds to drop a venom on the conquistadors which would cause them to rot. However, the *adelantado* invited Vitachuco to his camp; and after the exchange of many courtesies and vows of friendship, de Soto's men entered the cacique's deserted village. The Indians hidden in the woods discharged their arrows at the Spaniards the entire day; others remained in a cold lagoon where the water was so deep that, while three or four Indians swam, one stood on their backs so that he could shoot his arrows at the enemy. When the Indians, numb with the waters of the lagoon, refused to surrender, they were seized by Spaniards who swam after them and dragged them ashore, after which the Governor gave them mirrors and silks and sent them home. De Soto then invited the cacique to his table, and Vitachuco, who had an enormous, violent body, rose while his host was still eating and, seizing the *adelantado* by the neck, gave him a blow over the eyes, the mouth, and the nose. Then falling upon his prone and half-dead victim, he began to mangle de Soto until the Spaniards killed the savage.

Traveling for days with no food except grass and the tendrils of vines, the miserable band and their captain came to Cofachiqui. After receiving them, the princess of that realm removed a long necklace, the pearls of which were as large as hazelnuts, and gave it to de Soto. She then took them to her ancestral graveyard, where the dead were deposited in baskets woven out of cane. There were twenty-five thousand pounds of pearls in this charnel house, which were held of little worth by the Spaniards because they had been pierced by copper needles and the smoke had somewhat discolored them. Hernando do Soto had instructed his soldiers to make rosaries of the pearls, but all the pearls were lost or cast away.

The lady of Cofachiqui, a beauty with immense modesties, was asked to accompany the *adelantado*. The Inca said these brutish Dianas were very chaste, but when a Spaniard was caught by several Indian women, they gave him agonies by pounding his genital organs, and he either perished or suffered from another horrible affliction. On one of their marches the maiden Cofachiqui went into a thicket to relieve herself, and carrying a chest of pearls, escaped with a Moor from Barbary and two negro slaves.

After de Soto had perished in the wilderness, the Spanish remnant, of no more than three hundred, departed in boats that were miserable river huts and were pursued by Indians in canoes for a thousand miles down the Mississippi.

The European succumbed to the new continent; it was sterile earth which brewed fatal ends. Indian earth was a negative Golgotha. Martin Carvalho, a Portugal, went with over two hundred men in quest of gold, which is almost as indestructible as avarice. They came upon a crystal mountain and then saw a river between two mountains which shone like the stones of Ophir. They bit the grains with their teeth to determine whether it was a precious metal. In desert country their sustenance was some grass; one day they caught a snake upon which they supped. Sick and fearful of the red savages, they turned back in canoes, going on the River Cricare; in a rapid the canoe containing the gold was lost. After eight months of starvation, they returned to Porto Seguro utterly poor, their hopes dead.

The Spanish hidalgo and adventurer came for riches, but the loot was often no more than the piñon nut, tanned hides of the woolly cattle of the Platte, or virgin discovery, which, like learning, is tombstone destiny.

Beneath the crust of the Christian was the new earth and riparian heathen. The discoverers found wild ground that slaked their own natures. One ransacking customs to understand man is no less baffled than Montezuma was when, seeing Cortés and his soldiers kneeling to the Rood, he asked why they humbled themselves before an ordinary tree.

XII

Ginger, cassia, storax paint the Moluccas in the blood.
Magellan's men are glyphic bones at the Popinjays; the
ague breathes prayer into the visage as dotish as the penguin
in the Straits; pepper draws mirth from the Pole Antarctic.
Potosi, under the tropics, is desert rock, cold and grassless.

Magellan watered at the Isle of Thieves, lost rope, tackle,
a Portugal shirt, hawk's bells; he guerdoned the natives with
arrows they plucked as holy relics from the flesh, and, dying,
marveled how heaven drank their olive blood.

Men are milder on their knees, though ever chaffering with
doom shackled to chance. Gathering wrack in the windy

Magellans, the sole lodestar of sea-worn hearts was their daughters at Cádiz, and remembering these immaculate maids of their Andalusia, entered a wild tract of water, named it the Strait of the Eleven Thousand Virgins.

Man is just and energetic in battle, but at home sensual, a perjurer, and a malicious neighbor. The ten thousand Greeks were querulous and venal until they saw one of their men, betrayed by the Persian Tissaphernes, carrying the Greek's intestines in his hands.

Cyrus the younger had an ecstatic nature and could not taste the best of wine or of breads without sending partly emptied flagons of it or half-eaten loaves to his friends. Cyrus was a military seer; he so abhorred chicane, deceit, sloth, and injustice that any number of his soldiers were without hands, legs, and eyes. How can one account for the human mind? The Euphrates is one of the rivers in Paradise, but the Arabian plains along its banks are covered with wormwood.

At Hochelaga Jacques Cartier saw a savage with some pelts around his body which looked like the papyri that grow in the Nile but which were the skins of a foe. In northwest America the natives came to the ships of Captain Cook with the skulls and the hands of enemies which they sought to barter for iron and nails.

One cacique told Cartier of a region, a moon's journey from Hochelaga, laden with oranges and almonds, which are the fruits of desire that killeth the will. The Indians sowed miracles no less than Mandeville, and they mentioned a people born with one leg who voided nothing but water. But this was less of a prodigy than the throng of Indians, some senile, and others crippled or with diseased eyes, who came to be healed simply by touching Cartier.

Indian savages showed their love by stroking the breast of a stranger. When Cartier had looked for a place to disembark but could not, a barbarian swam to the vessel and, carrying Cartier to land, embraced him. At one of the islands in the South Seas, a dying soldier begged Magellan to give him a plaister of the intestines of a native for his fever. Wounded Spaniards took the fat of a slain Indian to assuage their own wounds.

The bowels of our foes cure us no less than those of our friends, for men, if peace is their yoke and boredom, can only clasp one another's hands when they are struggling together against their adversaries; for men apart are criminals and only together are sane.

The ground was vindictive; the savin, laurel, the alligator tree madden the faculties. At Canada the soldiers of Jacques Cartier were dying of a *Nueva Firma* plague; the teeth were cast out, the mouth fell away, and they had the stench of holy Lazarus in his grave. Opening the body of a youth just dead of the scurvy, they found the heart, which looked like milky quartz, and the water about it was the color of the jubilant Babylonian date. The dying French lay in the snows behind the palisades, fearing that the Indians would massacre all of them.

Cartier, meeting a savage, cured of the scurvy, furtively enquired how he had recovered. Without guile the Indian said he had cooked the bough of a spruce with its leaves and drunk the decoction every third day.

Ragged earth seldom produces mild men; the rivers of the New Continent are choleric, and the reason that the rapacious Scamander, with whom Achilles fought, appears to be small and of little importance is that Homer has tamed this stream.

The Viceroy Don de Luna y Arellano with an army of fifteen hundred soldiers set out to conquer the kingdom of Florida. After anchoring in a fine, halcyon bay, a hurricane broke the ships to pieces. A thousand survivors had no food until they came to a settlement called Nanipacna, where the corn was so harsh they had to soak it in sea water and then in fresh water to make it palatable. As there were not enough leaves, twigs, and bark for victuals, the men chewed the rawhide linings of their bucklers just as Aeneas and his companions kept themselves alive by gnawing their wooden trenchers. Summer chestnuts and the walnut tree sustained them for a fifty days' march to Olibahali, where they bartered beads and some cloth for vegetables, fruit, and corn.

The Spaniards found an aromatic to relieve them of pains, and they made a rosary of these herbs, which they carried around their necks. A Frenchman had discovered American sassafras, that has the odor of fennel, in which Prometheus hid the fire he had stolen from Zeus. Sassafras grows by the sea, and causes stones to pass, and was reckoned good for the pox. Perhaps, it is too marvelous an agony to suffer simply to discover fennel, sassafras, or to pursue the river tracks of the Cephisus to its source. Homer has no disdain, and the least he knows is poetry. Demeter ranged the whole earth in search of her daughter, Persephone, who plants hyacinth, violets, lupines, as she wanders.

Insolent Pelias paid for Jason's expedition to the River Phasis in Colchis. Menelaus, Ulysses, Jason, were the freebooters of the seas; Drake, Magellan, the Norse, were briny robbers. Martin Frobisher, covetous of ivory, electrum, and silver as Menelaus, came over the North Sea looking for the strait to China. He loaded his ship with the

Colchian precious metals, and when he returned, he found that he had a cargo of gravel. Frobisher had discovered estuaries, bays, isles, a channel that bears his name, and gravel, which is not all dross.

English voyagers had come to Nova Zembla, discovered by William Barents; their diet was deer, sea cows, bears, and the frozen seas. After eating bear's liver for a winter, all their hair fell out. Munck and his sailors had reached Nova Zembla, which is Russian for "New Land." Arctic hunger ruined their mouths and teeth; they dug up some kind of raspberry out of the ice and postponed dying. In the month of May geese, swans, little hoopoes, woodcocks, swallows, and falcons appeared, but they were too feeble to hunt them. Of Munck's crew of sixty-four sailors, two lived.

A Danish pilot happened upon a river of gold in Nova Zembla, and taking his cargo back to his homeland, there learned that he had carried a ship of sand across the Barents Sea. Tragedy is not so extreme a travail as folly; he died shortly afterward because, alive, he was ridiculous.

Majuelas was wrecked in Ascension Bay; the desolate shingle provided him snails and shellfish. At night he roosted in a tree and watched a tiger feeding upon a deer, and by dawn he ate what the tiger had left. At Cape Cotoch in Yucatán there was an edifice in the sea showing an idol whose flanks were being devoured by two ferocious animals; there was also a thick stone serpent that was swallowing a lion. Aguilar and his companions were cast on the coast of Yucatán; five of his men were sacrificed to the starved idols and others enslaved; all except two died grieving.

There were many martyrs of Canada and Florida, and the streams and towns that bear their names seem as apocryphal as the numerous towns of Jason that are everywhere in Armenia and in Media. The sea brigands who drowned in the Florida tides or in the Iroquois wilderness are as renowned as Juba, Ptolemy, and Aristotle; they were no worse than Jason, who was said by some to have gone far up the Ister, or even into the Exterior Sea. The Argonautic expedition was no less real than the fleets of Cristóbal Colón or Sir Walter Raleigh's quest for El Dorado in Guiana.

Freebooters like Jason who learned navigation from Aeolus came to America for the Golden Fleece, but most of them died mad or drowned in storms off the Bahamas. Magellan, bringing the Christian cross to the Moluccas, was a lunatic pirate; Frobisher was as greedy as Cacus, whom Hercules subdued. The Danes, reaching Greenland, found nothing but natives clothed in the skins of penguins and pelicans.

The friars murdered in the wilderness by an Iroquois hatchet were madmen; they kissed the stakes at which they were burnt; the Indians chewed the fingers of Father Jean Brebeuf until they were stumps, pulled out his lips and tongue, but he died without murmuring against his fate. Father Goupil died when the Indians hurled a tunic of hot chains on his naked body. Father Isaac Jogues, searching for the corpse of Goupil, found it had been eaten by dogs. Jogues returned to France, but he had such a wild zeal to bring the monstrance and the creed to the Iroquois that he came back to the Indian country, where one of these woodland brutes broke his skull with a hatchet. The diabolical Iroquois drank the blood of the monk Brebeuf to make them as brave as he. Each new century begets its perdition and mentor, and new ground, scarce weaned from Ocean, nursed the Iroquois. The annals of the race are writ in gore, a copious draught of which is titled erudition.

Fray Juan Ferrer and Padre Marcos de Mena walked naked on the shore of the Rio de los Palmas, in which two whales took their summer sleep. When the Indians returned with new arrows, they shot one into the back of Fray Juan, which killed him. The monk Marcos received seven wounds, and one of them was in his throat. He found his Spanish companions, but they were too feeble to carry him, and they buried him in the sand at the edge of the river, leaving his face uncovered so that he could breathe until he expired. Before the Spanish soldiers had reached the Panuco River, every one was slain by the Indians. The monk slept on the banks of the Tanipa, and when he awakened, the maggots were singing in his wounds. He had fallen into such a delirium that, when two Indians wrapped him in cotton blankets and carried him in a canoe to a Spanish town, he thought they were the angels whom Abraham saw beneath the terebinth at Mamre.

The friars who settled near the Canada River were Prometheans, and their malady was their desire to do good. The visionary attempts to shake the beast out of him; virtue sickens men. Those who endeavor to be just, not to lie, murder, or dupe others, are beside themselves, and they can find no friends in such a cause to be their companions. That Socrates was ill when he took the hemlock there can be no doubt; for he, like his pupil Plato, spent most of his days by the waters of Phlegethon, praying to Zeus and Hera and Hermes for death, for alive man is a liar, lecher, and thief, or else he shakes by the rivers of death.

Peter had scarce the courage to walk on water. One of the prophetic Isaiahs was said to have been sawed to pieces in the days of Manasseh, but this is an unbearable burden for the mind and drives the ghosts of all races to the furies. Seers, when they lived, were eremetic specters, who walked beside themselves, for men in this fell world are too cunning and wanton to keep them company.

Man is the animal who thinks, but he cannot employ his intellect without losing his reason, which is why Cristóbal Colón saw mermaids in the waters near the Antilles, or how Plato conceived the *Timaeus*. It would be doleful to imagine that the Golden Fleece were nothing else but the precious metals of Colchis or that Cortés, de Soto, Drake, Cook, Magellan, Cabot, seeking the strait to the khans of Tartary for nutmegs, gold, and emeralds, were not water-philosophers.

The Patagonians, living wretched, as though this were man's polestar, are gigantic boys and girls. The lives of the Chippeways, the Patagonians, the Fuegians, the Guaraunos are chronicles of lamentation, for all were once the sons of Apollo.

The footpath over the swift waters of the Apurimac was of osier; Daedalus could not have built the temples at Palenque or at Cuzco; the stones for the fanes and oratories at Cholula are said to have been seamed together without iron by the Toltecs or demigods. Papyrus was gathered in the Delta marshes, or by the waters at Byblos, and yet at the time of Martial and Vergil, the sacred paper from the Syrian seas or found at the Pelusiac mouth of the Nile was scarce, but abundant at Tabasco, Tenochtitlán and Mayapán. Montezuma, surrounded by concubines and enough gnomes and copal-smelling humpbacks to delight Domitian, craved gold, silver, and salves, and especially papyrus.

The Indians have many gentle traits; in Brazil the natives

devour their sick kindred because they have not so cruel a heart as to bury them and give them to a grub. There is no people more civil or timorous as those at Otaheite. When a father or mother died, the children beat their teeth with stones and thrust a shark's tooth into their heads until the blood poured upon them. They are a mild, pacific people and have no faults save thievery, which they do without skulking, and cannibalism. They have a humble deity by the name of Eatooa, whom they trundle in a hand-barrow. They are very pious, given to abundant but not grum prayers, and after they have plucked out the two eyes of the corpse slain to appease Eatooa, they wrap each eye in a green leaf.

The gods that enslave men the least are those that cannot be seen, painted, or imagined. The most didactic tombs are vacant, as the crypt of Ephesian John, which contains nothing except manna.

SIGNATURE is a new series of shorter works, distinguished by the highly personal and imaginative approach of the author to his subject. It will comprise works of poetry and prose, fiction and non-fiction, and will include English and American as well as authors of other nationalities in translation.

Signature 1
DARKER ENDS by Robert Nye *poems*

Signature 2
OLT by Kenneth Gangemi *novel*

Signature 3
THE CARNAL MYTH by Edward Dahlberg
essay

Signature 4
THE THEATRE AND ITS DOUBLE
by Antonin Artaud *essays*

Signature 5
SHARDS by Nick Rawson *prose poem*

Signature 6
ENEMIES by Reinhard Lettau *sketches*

Signature 7
REFLECTIONS by Mark Insingel *novel*

Signature 8
A BLACK MANIFESTO IN JAZZ, POETRY AND PROSE
by Ted Joans

Signature 9
LESSNESS by Samuel Beckett *prose*

Signature 10
STORIES FOR CHILDREN by Peter Bichsel
short stories